Unbelievable Desserts with Splenda

Also by Marlene Koch:

Fantastic Foods with Splenda:
160 Great Recipes for Meals Low in Sugar,
Carbohydrates, Fat, and Calories

50 Splenda Recipes:
Favorites from Fantastic Foods with Splenda
and Unbelievable Desserts with Splenda

Low-Carb Cocktails:
All the Fun and Taste Without the Carbs
(with Chuck Koch)

Unbelievable Desserts with Splenda

Sweet Treats Low in Sugar, Fat, and Calories

Marlene Koch

M. Evans and Company, Inc.
New York

M. Evans and Company, Inc.
216 East 49th Street
New York, New York 10017

Library of Congress Cataloging-in-Publication Data

Koch, Marlene.
    Unbelievable desserts with Splenda : sweet treats low in sugar, fat, and calories / by Marlene Koch.
       p.   cm.
    ISBN 0-87131-964-0
    1. Desserts. 2. Nonnutritive sweeteners. I. Title.
TX773 .K575 2001
641.8'6—dc21   2001040766

This book offers sweet treats to be enjoyed as part of an overall healthy diet and is not intended as a dietary prescription. Persons with health concerns should seek the advice of a qualified professional, such as a physician or registered dietitian, for a personalized diet plan. Even though the FDA has determined sucralose to be safe for everyone, persons consuming Splenda do so at their own risk. Neither the author nor the publisher is liable for the product and neither is in any way affiliated with the manufacturer, McNeil Specialty Products.

Splenda® is a registered trademark of McNeil Specialty Products Company, a Division of McNeil-PPc Inc.

Book design by Evan H. Johnston

Printed in the United States of America

20 19 18 17 16 15 14

Contents

To all those who strive to be healthy,
yet still want to indulge in the sweet things in life

Introduction

I'm going to just come out and say it; Splenda is an amazing substitute for sugar. For the first time, I can cook and bake with little or no sugar and produce delicious, sweet, satisfying treats. I'm not talking about pale imitations either, these are really delectable goodies that stand right up to their high-fat, full-sugar counterparts. Now that is amazing.

As a culinary nutritionist, I have made a career of developing recipes for great tasting, nutritious food. I believe that food that tastes good can actually be good for you. My goal is to create "food to die for—not from." Over the years, I have had the opportunity to teach chefs across the country the basics of creating wonderful healthy meals. In my cooking classes, I have been able to prove that it is possible to produce incredibly appetizing low-fat foods. But when the subject of lowering the sugar content in recipes—especially in baked goods—came up, I struggled. Sure, I knew all the standard techniques of increasing the spices, reducing the amount of sugar, and using items like fructose or juice concentrates to sweeten. But the truth was, these changes usually altered only the *type* of sugar; they did not drastically reduce the total sugar content. When the sugar content was truly lowered, the results no longer met my expectations of being really great treats.

Then, last October, I was asked to develop a class for the Columbus Culinary Academy that would feature solely low-sugar desserts. Since I had taught classes for the local Diabetes Association, Director and Chef Carolyn Claycomb was sure I could pull it off, but the thought of a teaching a class featuring only desserts low in fat and sugar made me a little nervous. After I got over my anxiety of wondering, "How will I wow them this time?" I got excited at the very idea of helping people who love desserts but need to lower the sugar content of all their favorites for health reasons. I searched high and low for the best low-sugar dessert recipes I could find. What I found was that there were a lot of "no sugar" cookbooks that were full of added sugars in the form of fructose, honey, and concentrated fruit juices. I also found many that used aspartame, saccharin, and other non-nutritive sweeteners as substitutes for sugar. I had tried using these substitutes myself, but found that they did not meet my quality standards. Lastly, there were a few sources that offered recipes for cold desserts, but what I really wanted to do was create true home-baked desserts—low-sugar versions of family favorites. But how?

I had heard there was a new non-nutritive sweetener called *sucralose* that might help me in creating recipes to meet my expectations, but I was unable to find it in any of the local markets. Just as I was about to give up, a friend told me about a new product called Splenda. It was just what I was looking for. After one try, I knew then that low-sugar baking could, at last, include healthy recipes that were every bit as attractive and delicious as their full-sugar counterparts. The day had come where I could indeed produce luscious, sweet, homebaked favorites that were low in both fat *and* sugar. Dessert would never be the same.

What is Splenda?

Splenda is the trade name for the revolutionary, new dietary sweetener sucralose. This non-nutritive (no calorie) sweetener is derived from sugar through a multistep patented process. A substitution of chlorine atoms for three of sugar's eight hydrogen-oxygen pairs results in a substance that tastes just like the sugar it is made from—without the calories. Since sucralose is 600 times sweeter than sugar, it is mixed with maltodextrin (a carbohydrate derived from corn), which provides volume and allows it to measure cup for cup like sugar. This product is Splenda Granular.

What is so amazing is that Splenda tastes like sugar. However, since the body does not recognize sucralose as sugar, it is not metabolized—thus, there are no calories. (Bulking agents provide a minute amount of carbohydrate calories—5 per tablespoon.) This also means it has no effect on blood sugar or the secretion of insulin. Studies focusing on persons with diabetes have confirmed this. Sucralose has been demonstrated to be safe for everyone.* Over one hundred scientific studies conducted over a twenty-year period have confirmed its safety. It has received approval for use in over thirty countries to date. In fact, you'll find no warning labels of any kind on Splenda.

With my science and health background, it is important to me that the products I choose are safe, but here is what really excites the culinarian in me:

- Splenda tastes great.
- Splenda has a long shelf life.
- Splenda has good solubility for beverages.
- Splenda does not have a bitter aftertaste, even when used in large quantities.
- Splenda retains its sweetness when heated, unlike other artificial sweeteners.
- You can bake with Splenda!

---

*Although Splenda is considered safe for everyone, pregnant women and children have special dietary needs that should be considered before adding sucralose to the diet. Consult your physician or a registered dietitian for advice.

Why Not Just Use Sugar?

Americans have an incredible sweet tooth. In fact, the affinity for sugar starts the day we're born. Ask any nurse the trick for getting a baby to take a bottle, and you may find that it's a touch of sugar water on the nipple. The truth is, a little added sugar in the diet is not a problem. Sugar is not evil. Sugar is actually a good source of energy, and sweet treats are certainly an enjoyable part of everyday living. Then why do the 2000 United States Department of Agriculture (USDA) Dietary Guidelines for Americans recommend that we moderate our intake of sugars?

The Problem with Sugar

First sugar promotes tooth decay. Second, sugar is full of calories—empty calories to be exact. Third, as added sugars* increase in the diet, either fewer calories are left for nutritious foods or weight gain occurs from the extra calories. In many sweet foods, with the exception of soda and some candies, sugar is often paired with fat and this is clearly not desirable if you are concerned about your weight. Additionally, a diet high in added sugars may also boost triglyceride levels and adversely affect your blood sugar levels. Again, not exactly desirable for maintaining good health.

How Much Sugar Is Too Much?

So what's a moderate intake of sugar? (See "Sugar—The Name Game," on page 18 for a listing of added sugars.) Most health organizations recommend that the average person consuming 2200 calories a day limit his or her sugar intake to 12 teaspoons a day (10 percent or less of your total calories).

Let's put that into perspective: A can of regular soda pop has 10 to 12 teaspoons of sugar, as do many pre-sweetened coffee drinks. A four-ounce muffin has 8 to 10 teaspoons, a piece of frosted carrot cake has 12 teaspoons, and a piece of *"light"* restaurant cheesecake can have as much as 14 teaspoons of sugar. Is it any surprise that we are consuming 170 pounds of sugar per year (per person) in the United States?

---

*Sugars that occur naturally in foods are not considered "added" and are not usually a concern for healthy individuals.

On a daily basis, we average 20 teaspoons of added sugar, twice the recommended amount. That adds up to a whopping 110,000 calories a year—the caloric equivalent of thirty extra pounds!

How Splenda Can Help

Desserts and sweetened beverages are by far the greatest contributors of added sugars in our diets. By using non-caloric sweeteners, such as sucralose, to replace sugars when possible, we can still enjoy the sweet treats we love without the extra sugar and calories. Splenda has only 96 calories per cup instead of sugar's 775. Now we really can have our cake and eat it too!

Diabetes

What is Diabetes?

My stepdaughter has type 2 diabetes. Since her diagnosis, Colleen has made many lifestyle changes. She has lost weight, watches the choices and portion sizes of the food she eats, and tries to get some exercise, but she has *not* lost her love for all the delicious sweet things in life. For her and the other 16 million Americans that have diabetes, sugar is an issue. Diabetes is a serious disease that affects the body's ability to metabolize glucose. Glucose is a type of sugar that is produced when either sugars or starches in any form are eaten. Insulin, a hormone secreted by the pancreas, is necessary for the body to utilize glucose for energy. In persons with diabetes, the body does not produce insulin, does not produce enough insulin, and/or the insulin does not work efficiently enough (due to insulin resistance of the cells). Without the proper amount of insulin, glucose (or sugar in the blood) accumulates above normal levels. This can have negative consequences, in both the short and long term. For the person with diabetes, a healthy diet and sensible meal planning are important tools in managing their blood sugar levels.

Does Having Diabetes Mean You Can't Eat Sugar?

It was once believed that persons with diabetes needed to eliminate all sugar from the diet. We now know that the rate at which a particular food affects the blood sugar depends on a lot of factors, and not simply its sugar content.* Based on this knowledge, new guidelines for diabetes management have been set forth by both the American Diabetes and Dietetic Associations. The emphasis is on the *total amount* and *quality* of the carbohydrate (carbs) one eats. Sugar can now be used as part of an overall healthy diet—and that's great news if you have diabetes and you love sweets.

---

* The measurement of a food's effect on insulin and blood sugar levels is called its *glycemic index*. This is sometimes used to aid food selection for controlling weight and blood sugar.

As usual, there's a catch. When you consider a healthy diet that provides you with all of the nutrients you need, without excessive total calories and especially carbs, there just isn't much room for a lot of added sugar. Especially since most people with type 2 diabetes need to reduce calories, not add more to their diets.

Great Sweet Treats for Persons with Diabetes

Which brings me back to my stepdaughter—every day is a balance of good choices and good taste. Desserts, treats, sweet beverages—Colleen wants to enjoy them like everybody else. That means goodies that really taste like her old time favorites, not just "diet treats." She also enjoys having a whole piece of something (sometimes even more). She is delighted that I can now prepare many of her favorite foods and drinks again. Birthdays are no problem—I can make chocolate cake. Holidays are no problem—we can make pumpkin pie. Picnics are no problem—she can have a couple of chocolate chip cookies. Since Splenda has almost no calories and doesn't affect blood sugar, using Splenda in low-fat recipes gives you the flexibility to meet your nutrition goals and, more importantly, to enjoy it!

Do You Really Need to Lower the Fat?

I recently saw a so-called "nutrition expert" on television say that cutting the sugar out of your diet was *all* it took to stay slim and healthy. If that were true, it would be easy for me to put together rich tasting, good-for-you treats. In fact, I've seen recipes based on this premise: cream cheese, whipping cream, eggs, and sugar substitutes were the ingredients for a cheesecake. The sugar and carbohydrate content was low, but the fat load was outrageous. I analyzed one recipe. It contained 40 grams of fat per serving, which made up 93 percent of the calories. You may as well sit down and eat half a stick of butter!

Fat Facts

No matter what the hype, the following facts have been scientifically proven to be true:

- Calories do count.
- Fat is dense in calories.
- A diet high in saturated fat is not good for you.

Lower Fat—Better Health

Most likely, if you're looking to reduce the added sugar in your diet, you want to lose weight, control your blood sugar, or improve your health. In each of these cases, consuming a lot of fat is not going to help you. Here's why:

- Fat is full of calories. Need proof? One gram of fat equals 9 calories, whereas carbohydrate and protein have only 4 calories per gram. Many studies have been done on what it takes to gain or lose weight and here is the truth: If you consume more calories than you burn, you will gain weight, but if you burn more than you consume, you will lose weight. It's that simple. High-fat diets are often higher in calories, because foods high in fat have a lot of calories. Period. When you trim the fat, you trim the calories.

- Fat can contribute to an increase in insulin resistance. It's true that when it comes to controlling your blood sugar, a *little* fat can actually be helpful. It doesn't create much of an insulin response, and it can help to slow the rise in blood sugar when it is eaten with foods high in carbohydrate. For example, ice cream has a lower glycemic index than sherbet; however, a rich ice cream has almost twice the calories. Those extra calories are important, because if you have diabetes and are overweight (as are 80 percent of persons with type 2 diabetes), losing weight is often a priority. Research shows that both abdominal fat and saturated fats in the diet can increase insulin resistance. So again, fat loses.

- Saturated fat has been implicated in increasing the risk for certain cancers as well as heart disease. For those persons with diabetes, this is of particular concern because they are at high risk for heart disease. Does all this mean that fat, not sugar, is the evil one and we can't have any? Of course not.

How much fat is too much?

Looking at the USDA Dietary Guidelines for Americans once more, the recommendation is to consume no more than 30 percent of your total calories as fat, with less than than 10 percent from saturated fat. In many weight loss programs, physicians and registered dietitians suggest no more than 25 percent of your calories should come from fat. For that average person consuming 2200 calories, this would allow for a total intake of 61 to 73 grams of fat per day. (Remember, that means *all* your meals and snacks) Currently, the American diet is closer to 34 percent than the maximum 30 percent recommended. That 4-percent difference adds up to a lot of added calories and pounds every year. How do some favorite treats measure up? Well, a large muffin has 24 grams of fat, a brownie has 27 grams, a sticky bun at Mrs. Fields has 34 grams, and a piece of restaurant cheesecake has 50 grams. It might not be so bad if these foods were offering you a lot of nutrients, but they aren't.

Low-Fat Yet Luscious

I'm particularly proud of the fact that even though I've managed to re-create many favorites—like carrot cake and cheesecake, chocolate chip cookies and coconut cream pie, and even some amazing cream puffs—that are low in fat (as well as in sugar and calories), they are still delicious. You'll be pleasantly surprised when you taste these treats, because although they are low in fat, you'd never know it by tasting them.

How to Interpret the Nutritional Analysis

The nutrition information that follows each of the recipes in this book has been calculated using Esha Nutrition Food Processor software. The nutrient content has been provided to help you make choices appropriate to your own needs and goals. Here are four points, along with my personal philosophy about the calculation of the nutritional information:

1. Real Portions

I have a real problem with healthy recipes that look "healthy" because the portion size is ridiculous. No, I'm not talking restaurant size, "I could barely finish it" ridiculous, I'm talking ridiculous as in miniscule. Portion size is an issue and we've all gotten a little too used to today's out of control, bigger-is-better mentality, but I have also seen dessert portions the size of a postage stamp in some popular healthy cookbooks and magazines. Okay, I'm exaggerating, but realistically, I have seen portions of cake cut smaller than the size of a credit card. I have found very few people satisfied with portions *that* small. Therefore, I have tried to find the middle ground: A 9-inch pie serves eight, a 9-inch cheesecake serves twelve, and a square cake pan of 8 or 9 inches is cut into 3 × 3-inch servings for cakes and no smaller than 3 × 5-inches for bar cookies. (I actually saw one recipe that yielded thirty-six bar cookies out of this size pan.)

2. Fat by the Numbers

Although I have previously mentioned the percentage of calories that should come from fat in foods, fat-percentage calculations in Splenda products need to be viewed differently. Fat percentage is a mathematical calculation: To calculate the percentage of fat in a product you divide the calories that come from fat by the *total* number of calories. For example, if a muffin has 15 grams of fat—which equals 135 calories from fat (15 grams × 9 calories per gram = 135)—and a total of 400 calories, the fat percentage would be 34 percent (135 fat calories ÷ 400 total calories = .34, or 34 percent). Thus, the greater the total calories, with fat remaining the same, the lower the fat percent will be. Raise the calories to

500 and you will see the fat percentage drops (135 ÷ 500 = .27 or 27 percent). In fact, food manufacturers have been known to increase the sugar or carbohydrate in a product—instead of lowering the fat—to bring the fat percentage to or below 30 percent in order to call a food low-fat! What happens when you use Splenda is that the total number of calories goes down. That's good, but because the reduction is all from carbohydrate, it can make the fat *percentage* look high. A good example would be the Lemon Chiffon Pie. There are 170 (luscious) calories per piece; 60 of them come from fat—that's 35 percent. If I were to use sugar, the calories would be 240, and the fat calories would still be 60. Now my pie is 25 percent fat, but the carbohydrate grams would double and the grams of sugar would triple! The bottom line is that all the recipes have acceptable levels of fat for maintaining good health and great taste. Their caloric content is significantly reduced from their full-fat counterparts, and both total fat and saturated fat are low.

3. Exchanges and Carbohydrate Counting

I have used the most current guidelines available to calculate the diabetic exchanges. You will find the exchanges rounded off to the nearest half. This was decided after consulting with the Director of Nutrition Services and Certified Diabetes Educator for the Central Ohio Diabetes Association. She and I both feel that counting should be made easy, not confounding. I think you will be really amazed at how few exchanges you have to use to get real pieces of real desserts. I have been a nutritionist for many years and these counts genuinely impress me. Of course, the total carbohydrate grams along with fiber are available for those counting carbs. I also included the actual sugar grams for those who are especially trying to reduce their intake of simple sugars. If you are concerned with the glycemic index of a food, remember that fat, fiber, and protein, when mixed with carbohydrate, all lower the glycemic index. A piece of pie that is moderate in fat and sugar will have a lower glycemic index than a very low-fat dessert that is high in sugar.

4. Desserts are a lot More than Numbers

This the final word—relax. Peek at the numbers, but more importantly, enjoy. This is not meant to be a "diet" book but a book offering you an array of delectable treats that make eating fun! There isn't an item in this book that cannot be part of your healthy diet. How sweet is that?

Sugars—Sweeteners and So Much More

Sugar—The Name Game

Before I can talk about what sugar does, you need to know what sugar is. When most people hear the term "regular sugar," they think of refined white sugar or sucrose. Sucrose is a simple carbohydrate and is the most commonly used sweetener. Sucrose includes both refined white and less refined brown sugars. But when bakers, nutritionists, or the USDA speak of *sugars*, they are referring to the wide variety of sweeteners found naturally in foods as well as the sugars added during food processing. That is what you will find on the sugar line of a food label and in the analysis of the recipes in this book. For instance, in my Apple Pie in a Bag recipe (page 71), no sugar (sucrose) is added, but it still contains 13 grams of sugar, because apples—like other fruits and milk products—contain natural sugars. However, when we talk of curbing our intake of *added sugars*, we are speaking of all the simple sugars that we, not mother nature, add to foods. Added sugars include *brown sugar, confectioner's sugar, corn syrup, fructose, fruit juice concentrates, glucose, honey, molasses, raw sugar, table sugar,* and *syrups*. This means that the "all-fruit" pie sweetened with concentrated fruit juice is actually quite high in added sugars! Marketers love to take advantage of the fact that only sucrose (whether refined like white sugar or less refined like brown sugar) is listed as sugar on food packages.

The Role of Sugars in Baking

The truth is that many types of simple carbohydrate or sugars are used to sweeten the treats we all love. In addition to sweetening, sugars or caloric sweeteners play many other roles in making recipes "work." Sugars:

- Aid in texture, structure, and/or volume.
- Add color by browning.
- Impart flavor.
- Give spread to cookies and thickness to sauces.
- Stabilize egg whites in meringues and egg foams.
- Enhance the appearance of the finished products.
- Provide a natural preservative quality by holding moisture.
- Give moistness and tenderness.

In baking, the type of sugar selected for a recipe is based not only on its ability to sweeten, but the necessity for it to provide these additional functions for a particular desired outcome, *i.e.*, you pick the type of sweetener based on what you need it to *do* in the recipe. When it comes to low-sugar cooking and baking, *Splenda is excellent at sweetening.* It performs this particular function beautifully. Splenda is made from sugar and therefore tastes like sugar. The Granular measures cup-for-cup like sugar and has no aftertaste (unlike saccharin), and it can take the heat (unlike aspartame). In beverages, cheesecakes, fruit pies, and many cold desserts, little modification (beyond lowering the fat content) was necessary to achieve wonderful results. That is because the main role of sugar in these types of recipes is to sweeten.

However, since Splenda is not a traditional sugar but a non-nutritive sweetener, additional adjustments needed to be made when working with many recipes. Although each recipe is unique, after working with Splenda, I found there are some routine modifications that are helpful in order to get great results in low-sugar, low-fat baking which I have outlined on pages 24–25 in "Low Sugar Baking Secrets."

Real Desserts Incredibly Low in Sugar

My goal is to create great-tasting, eye-appealing, healthful desserts that you will enjoy eating and be proud to serve. Many times, it is not possible to do so without *any* sugar of *any* type. I have been highly selective in using additional sugars in small quantities in recipes as needed. When they are used primarily for eye appeal, I have noted them as (optional) on the recipes. Because I have used them judiciously and have confirmed that the additional carbohydrate is minimal, I have already *included* these garnishes in the analysis of the recipes. Until Splenda, I did not think it was possible to eliminate the quantity of sugar normally contained in these recipes with such great results. I think you will agree, like my tasters, that to have delicious treats like these with a mere fraction of the usual added sugars is amazing.

The Real Facts About Fats

Know Your Fats

There are different types of fats just as there are different types of sugars. Unlike the various sugars, which affect the body similarly, fats are far from considered alike. Mono- and polyunsaturated fats are considered to be more healthful in the diet than saturated fat or trans fatty acids, which are often labeled as the "bad fats." In order to maintain your health, it is recommended that you limit the total amount of fat you eat. Equally important is to consume the types of fats that are more healthful. Since saturated fat is one of the least desirable when it comes to your health, saturated fat gets its own line on the food label and is provided in the analysis of these recipes. You can compare for yourself the differences between commonly used fats by referring to the chart below:

Fat Facts

Fat Source	Amount	Calories	Total Fat*	Saturated Fat*	Monounsaturated Fat*	Polyunsaturated Fat*	Cholesterol†
Canola oil	1 Tbs	120	13.6	0.9	7.6	4.5	0
Safflower oil	1 Tbs	120	13.6	1.2	1.6	10.1	0
Corn oil	1 Tbs	120	13.6	1.7	3.3	8.0	0
Margarine (Regular Stick)	1 Tbs	101	11.4	1.8	6.6	2.4	0
Margarine (70% Veg. Oil)	1 Tbs	90	10.0	2.0	3.0	3.0	0
Shortening	1 Tbs	106	12.0	3.2	5.7	3.3	0
Butter	1 Tbs	102	12.2	7.2	3.3	0.4	33

*in grams
†in milligrams

You may notice that all fats contribute similar calories. In fact, oils actually have more calories per tablespoon than shortening or butter. You may also note that butter, one of the most loved ingredients in baking, contains the highest amount of saturated fat.

The Role of Fats in Baking

Despite its unhealthful qualities, butter is often a baker's number one choice because it has the best flavor of all baking fats. But fats also have many functions beyond their flavor. Fats:

- Give moistness and tenderness.
- Add flakiness to pastries.
- Carry other flavors.
- Are important for beating air into batters.
- Add smoothness.
- Contribute to "mouthfeel," providing that "melt in your mouth" sensation.

Solid fats, like butter and shortening, add different qualities to a recipe than liquid fats, like oil. For instance, while healthy oils are good for moistening, they cannot aerate, melt, or provide flakiness like solid fat. When reducing the total amount of fat, it is especially important that the fat you choose can do what you need it to do. This means sometimes using a healthy margarine when you need a solid fat, and sometimes even using a touch of butter when it can make a real taste difference. It also means choosing oil when moistness is the key and choosing shortening for a pie crust that is flaky, not tough. Whereas the fat can all but be eliminated in some recipes, in others, like cookies and pie crusts, some fat is clearly necessary to give a good quality product.

There are lots of ways to reduce or switch the type of fat used when baking. You will find many ideas and techniques in the "Low-Fat Baking Tips" section on page 23. You'll also notice substitutions made using dairy products. While not technically classified as fat, dairy products can contain a lot of fat. The technique *not* used, of course, is the addition of extra sugar to make up for the reduction in fat, a trick often used by food manufacturers.

Fabulous Desserts with Less Fat (and Sugar)

Please read the "About the Recipes" section that follows before you begin making the recipes. It will give you many tips and a better understanding of the modifications necessary to make these wonderful treats. Go ahead, it's your turn to splurge!

About the Recipes

Measuring and Baking Basics

In order to help you get the best results from these recipes, I have included the following list of helpful hints. Because exact measurements and cooking temperatures are crucial to the success of baking, more than in any other area of cooking, it is important that you follow the recipe instructions carefully. Read this section thoroughly before you begin.

Measure Accurately
Use dry measuring cups for heavy, wet, or sticky ingredients like applesauce, yogurt, and molasses. Dry ingredients should be measured level with the top of the measuring cup or spoon by using a knife to sweep away the excess. It is important to loosen or aerate the flour first by stirring it with a spoon. Brown sugar should be packed firmly into the measuring spoon or cup.

Use a clear glass measuring cup for liquids. To get an accurate reading, make sure the cup is placed on the counter and read at eye level.

Preheat Your Oven
Never begin baking in an oven that has not been brought up to the temperature specified in the recipe. Preheating only takes 15 or 20 minutes. This important step should never be overlooked because it can literally make the difference between your recipe succeeding or failing. If you are unsure about the accuracy of your oven, invest in an oven thermometer.

Cool Baked Goods Thoroughly
Use a rack for cooling to prevent excess condensation from forming on the bottom of baked goods.

Store Baked Goods Properly
Wrap completely with plastic wrap or foil, or store in air-tight containers after they are thoroughly cooled. Most homemade baked goods will maintain their quality for two to three days when properly wrapped. Cheesecakes can maintain their quality for several days stored in the refrigerator.

To freeze, wrap cooled items tightly in plastic or foil before freezing. Thaw frozen items completely before unwrapping. Thawed baked goods can be heated in the microwave or oven to refresh them before serving. Muffins, quick breads, and plain cakes freeze well.

Low-Fat Baking Tips

Lowering the fat in recipes without compromising taste is the goal of good low-fat baking. Eliminating *all* the fat is not the goal (although occasionally you can). I have lowered the fat in these recipes to healthy levels using the following tips. If you choose to make other substitutions in the recipes your results will vary.

- The type of fat (butter, margarine, oil, etc.) used in a recipe is important to that recipe. Each has its own pluses and minuses in cooking as well as in your health. (See pages 20–21, "The Real Facts About Fat.") I use butter when the flavor greatly contributes to the recipe or when the amount is so small that the nutritional difference is negligible. Margarine can usually be substituted for butter to lower the saturated fat and cholesterol. Substituting oil for solid fats when they are specified is not recommended.

- Low-fat dairy products are richer and usually better tasting than non-fat, but some light products are still quite high in fat (like Neufchâtel cheese). In order to get the best outcome and still have the recipe be healthful, I often mix non-fat and low-fat ingredients together. You may choose to splurge further and use all low-fat products or even use some higher-fat ones. You can do so without affecting the recipe. I do not, however, recommend that the recipes be made with all non-fat products unless specified.

- Fruit purées like applesauce, prune, pumpkin, and banana work well in adding moistness without fat. Although fruit purées do add some carbohydrate, their natural sugars also help low-sugar baked goods rise. As a rule of thumb, fruit purées can easily replace one-half the usual fat in a recipe. Applesauce works best in lighter tasting recipes, and prune purée gives great results in foods with stronger flavors—especially with chocolate. (I guarantee no one will ever know there are prunes hiding in any of these recipes!)

- Egg yolks add richness to recipes, but also contain cholesterol and saturated fat. Therefore, I have minimized the use of egg yolks, using them only as necessary. The current guidelines for healthy egg consumption have been relaxed and allow up to one whole egg daily. Because I prefer the natural taste of whole eggs for baking, I use egg whites (no fat or cholesterol here) instead of egg substitutes. If you prefer, you may use a quarter-cup of egg substitute to replace two whites or one whole egg in recipes that do not require the egg white to be whipped.

- You may find the amount of spices and extracts in these recipes to be more than you would normally use. Fats give flavor and carry flavorings in foods, thus the additional spices and extracts in reduced-fat recipes ensure full-flavored treats and desserts.

Low Sugar Baking Secrets

Please note that all the recipes in the book have been developed to work with the reduction of sugar and the use of Splenda Granular only. The following secrets will help you to understand the science behind these recipes as well as to how to make the adjustments required to invent your own true low-sugar, high-quality sweet treats using Splenda. Since other non-nutritive sweeteners are not chemically identical to Splenda, they cannot be substituted for Splenda with the same results in every case. Nor can the Splenda packets (see Splenda entry on page 28).

Secret #1
Sugar is sugar is sugar. Honey, juice concentrates, fructose—all sugars. Don't be fooled by that "no sugar cookie" full of honey. Your body knows what sugars are and so should you. See page 18 for the reason manufacturers can make these claims and a listing of the different types of added sugars.

Secret #2
A goal of *no* sugar in a dessert recipe is like there being no sand at the beach. That said, there are actually many great recipes in this book where no sugar of any kind has been added. However, there are also many recipes that use small amounts of different types of sugars. These sugars serve many functions beyond sweetening and although the amounts are very small, they have been deemed necessary for a good quality outcome. Additional reductions may be detrimental to the quality of the recipes. (See "The Role of Sugars in Baking," page 18.)

Secret #3
Sugar imparts volume to recipes. Since Splenda does not have the bulk of sugar, the volume and the weight of some recipes may be less. Adjustments need to be made to other ingredients (adding more), the pan size (using a smaller one), or in the case of drop cookies, the yield (making less), to make up for the loss of sugar.

Secret #4
When converting traditional recipes to low-sugar versions, you may need to adjust the leavening. The manufacturer recommends ½ teaspoon of baking soda be added for each cup of Splenda. In recipes that already had a significant amount of baking soda, I adjusted the baking powder instead. Baking soda is high in sodium, which can affect flavor in high quantities.

Secret #5
Baked goods made with Splenda will cook faster. Check cakes up to 10 minutes sooner, muffins 5 to 8 minutes sooner, and cookies 3 to 5 minutes sooner.

Secret #6
Drop cookies made with Splenda may not flatten as readily. Simply flatten them on the baking pan with the bottom of a glass or spatula before placing them in the oven.

Secret #7
Since Splenda doesn't brown like sugar, the addition of small amounts of brown sugar, honey, or molasses will help in browning as well as contributing flavor. Some baked items may simply be lighter in color than their traditional counterparts.

Secret #8
In recipes that have very little added sugar, the surface or crust can appear dull. To create a winning appearance, sprinkle the surface with a touch of granulated sugar before baking or powdered sugar after baking. Two teaspoons of sugar can coat an entire cake or batch of muffins, adding less than 1 gram of carbohydrate per serving.

Secret #9
Use small amounts of cornstarch to help thicken sauces that depend on sugar as the thickening agent.

Secret #10
Some recipes are not as successful when converted to low-sugar versions. It is difficult to replace regular sugar when large amounts are required for volume and structure (such as angel food cake, pound cake, meringue cookies), carmelization (such as candies and caramel sauces), or texture (pecan pie or cracked sugar toppings).

Ingredients That You Will Need

When creating low-sugar, low-fat treats, the exact combination of ingredients is crucial for great quality. Although you can make some substitutions in these recipes, you should use the ingredients specified in the recipe to ensure your treats taste as good as mine did, and that the nutritional information I have supplied is accurate.

Applesauce

Always use unsweetened applesauce. The sweetened varieties contain significant amounts of added sugar.

Buttermilk

Regular buttermilk is low in fat. I use buttermilk labeled low-fat, but regular and non-fat varieties are also fine. The acidity of buttermilk helps to tenderize baked goods and this is especially important when the fat and sugar in a recipe are low. You may also use powdered buttermilk, or you can substitute sour milk for buttermilk. To make sour milk, add 1 tablespoon of vinegar or lemon juice to a 1-cup measuring cup. Add skim or 1% milk to fill the cup. Let stand for 3 minutes before using.

Cake Flour

Cake flour has less protein than all-purpose flour. Fat and sugar both help to tenderize the protein in flour by inhibiting gluten formation. Because my cake recipes contain less fat and sugar, using cake flour produces a lighter, more tender cake. You'll find cake flour in the supermarket next to the flour; it's usually packaged in a box. The closest substitution would be to replace 2 tablespoons of each cup of all-purpose flour with cornstarch.

Cocoa Powder

Dutch-processed cocoa powder is cocoa powder that has had some of the natural acidity of cocoa neutralized. It brings a darker, smoother cocoa flavor to recipes. I use Hershey's European found on the baking aisle, but any brand is fine. You may substitute regular unsweetened cocoa powder, but the cocoa flavor may be less smooth in the finished product.

Cream Cheese

I use Philadelphia cream cheese. The light cream cheese is sold in a tub. You can substitute Neufchâtel cheese with good results, but it is higher in calories and fat. I also use Philadelphia non-fat cream cheese sold in an 8-ounce block. Mixing non-fat and low-fat cream cheeses together lowers the fat content, while still providing good flavor.

Eggs
I use pasteurized eggs in recipes where the egg white is not cooked long enough to ensure complete safety from the risk of salmonella poisoning. (There is always a slight risk of salmonella poisoning when eating uncooked eggs.) Whole eggs, pasteurized in their shell, are now available in most markets. I use Davidson's Pasteurized Eggs.

Flavorings
Real vanilla extract makes a difference, as do good-quality spices. Check your spices. If you can't smell them when you open the container, they are too old and should be replaced.

Low-Sugar Jam
I have specified low-sugar jam because it contains no non-nutritive sweeteners, has half the sugar of regular jam, and has a wonderful fruit taste. The brand I have used is Smucker's. All-Fruit spreads often contain concentrated fruit juices as sweeteners and are usually higher in sugar content (up to twice as much).

Margarine and Butter
You may substitute your own favorite brand. The margarine I used is 70% vegetable oil/buttermilk blend stick margarine. I like the Land O Lakes brand. Don't use margarine that contains less than 70 percent fat by weight, because they have a high water content and might ruin the recipe. Tub margarines are in this category. Light butter has all the flavor with half of the fat of regular butter. Use only when specified as it has a high water content.

Milk
I have specified 1% milk. At 20 percent fat, 1% milk fat is richer tasting than skim, without the fat of 2% or whole milk. Skim milk can be substituted if you'd like.

Nonfat Half-and-Half
Nonfat or fat-free half-and-half has the creamy richness of half-and-half without the fat. Because it has more carbohydrate than regular half-and-half, I use it in small amounts. Land O Lakes is the brand I have found. You can substitute regular half-and-half in the recipes; the grams of fat will be slightly higher. Do not substitute nonfat milk.

Nonstick Cooking Sprays
There are two types of oil-based sprays I specify for coating pans. The first is a vegetable oil spray made from canola or corn that is unfla-

vored, such as regular PAM. Be sure not to use an olive oil spray for baking, because the flavor is too strong. The second type is nonstick *baking spray* which contains a small amount of flour in the spray. This spray is great for cakes and other items that call for pans to be greased *and* floured. I use Baker's Joy.

Orange and Lemon Zest

Many recipes call for grated lemon or orange rind (zest). Simply grate the brightly colored outer layer off of the whole fruit. Use a box or sharp flat grater that has small holes to make a finely grated, but not mushy, zest. If the grated zest does not look finely minced, use a knife to finish it off before adding to the recipe. Try not to use too much of the bitter white pith beneath the colored layer.

Prune Purée

For prune purée I use a product called Sunsweet Lighter Bake found on the baking aisle of most stores. It is actually a combination of prunes and apples. Baby food prunes can also be used. You can also purée 1⅓ cups pitted prunes with 6 tablespoons of hot water until smooth to make your own purée. This will make 1 cup. Kept covered in the refrigerator it holds for 1–2 months. One tablespoon of purée replaces two tablespoons of fat in a recipe.

Splenda

Splenda can be found in most grocery stores stocked next to the sugar, or ordered directly from www.splenda.com. Splenda is available in the bulk form (Splenda Granular) or in packets. For baking, the granular is easier to pour and measure and each box contains approximately 4½ cups. *Please note: The recipes in this book were formulated using Splenda Granular although Splenda packets may be substituted in the beverage recipes only (3 packets = 2 tablespoons).*

Whipped Topping

Light whipped topping is found in tubs in the freezer section of supermarkets; be sure to thaw them before using. The non-fat versions of these toppings are not recommended because they have a higher sugar content.

Yogurt

Plain low-fat yogurt may be substituted for the non-fat variety. Otherwise, use only the type of yogurt specified. If regular low-fat yogurt is specified, do not substitute "light" yogurt or artificially sweetened yogurts. The sweetness does not always hold up in baking. The recipes that do contain sweetened yogurt serve twelve, so the amount of sugar in each portion is minimal.

Hot and Cold Beverages

*I*ce cold lemonade, steaming hot chocolate, fresh fruit smoothies. There are times when the perfect thing to hit the spot is not something to eat at all—but something to drink. The choices today in beverages are astounding. Every week there's a new kind of beverage to choose from. Coffeehouses, smoothie bars, and lemonade stands always seem to be there just when you're ready for a little something. Unfortunately, a recent study from Purdue University indicates that when it comes to calories and extra pounds, those little somethings really add up. It seems that consuming fluid calories doesn't give us the same sense of fullness that comes from eating solid food, so we wind up consuming extra calories that quickly add up. And since most of the calories in these beverages come from sugar or fat, you're also not getting much nutrition bang for your buck. If you enjoy these drinks, here are some great recipes for all your favorites. Best of all, these creations will definitely satisfy like their calorie-laden cousins because they taste just like them.

Since Splenda dissolves easily, can take the heat, and has no aftertaste, it is the perfect sugar replacement for these beverages. In fact, these beverages are so low in calories, fat, and sugar, you'll still have room to eat some of the other goodies in the book. So drink up.

Ice Cold Lemonade
Deep, Dark Hot Chocolate
Krista's Spiced Tea
Creamy Iced Coffee
Frosty Mocha
Strawberry Banana Smoothie
Berry Blast Smoothie
Orange Sunshine Smoothie

Ice Cold Lemonade

*N*othing beats the heat like cold lemonade. Unfortunately, the amount of
sugar it takes to sweeten those lemons is enough to make you pucker. So
enjoy this sweet version without the added calories.

1/3	cup fresh lemon juice (one large lemon) or 1/3 cup lemon juice concentrate
2	Tbs Splenda
	crushed ice

Pour the lemon juice into a tall (12 ounce) glass. Add the Splenda and stir
until dissolved. Add ice to fill the glass. Add water and stir. *One serving.*

Per serving:

Calories 30
Carbohydrate 9 grams (sugar 3)
Protein 0 grams
Diabetic exchange = 1/2 fruit

Fat 0 grams
Fiber 0 grams
Sodium 0 grams

Make this with fresh lemon juice and you
get 60% of your day's worth of vitamin C.

Deep Dark Hot Chocolate

*M*y eight-year-old son loves *his hot chocolate. After tasting what he now calls "Mom's special recipe," no other will do. There are a lot of specialty sugar-free hot chocolate mixes you can now buy, but they all lack a rich chocolate flavor. Now you can ward off the chills with a rich, dark cup of luscious hot chocolate that no packaged mix can match.*

(This also makes great cold chocolate milk—no heating required)

I	**Tbs unsweetened Dutch-process cocoa powder (like Hershey's European)**
I	**Tbs + 2 tsp Splenda**
2	**Tbs hot water**
I	**cup I% milk**

Place the cocoa powder and Splenda into a microwaveable mug. Add the hot water and stir until smooth. Pour in the milk and stir again. Microwave on high for 1½ minutes or until hot. (Do not boil.) *One serving.*

Flavor variations: Try adding ¼ teaspoon of vanilla, orange, or raspberry extract.

Per serving:

Calories 120
Carbohydrate 16 grams (sugar 11)
Protein 9 grams
Diabetic exchange = 1 low fat milk

Fat 3 grams (saturated 2)
Fiber 1 gram
Sodium 124 milligrams

> Did you know that individual packets of hot chocolate can contain 5 teaspoons of sugar?

Krista's Spiced Tea

A friend and colleague of mine is the Nutritional Services Director for the Central Ohio Diabetes Association. She was kind enough to give me the recipe for a hot tea that she and her clients really enjoy. This tea reminds me of hot cider, but has fewer calories and no added sugar in it. It is great on its own, but would go especially well with the goodies in the next chapter.

3	cups of boiling water
3	cinnamon stick tea bags
1/2	cup unsweetened orange juice
1	teaspoon lemon juice
1/3	cup Splenda

Steep tea bags in water for 5 minutes. Remove tea bags and discard. Add orange juice, lemon juice, and Splenda. Stir and serve. *Four servings.*

Variation: Serve cold with ice.

Per serving:

Calories 15
Carbohydrate 4 grams (sugar 2)
Protein 0 grams
Diabetic exchange = 1 free serving

Fat 0 grams
Fiber 0 grams
Sodium 0 milligrams

This tea smells wonderful. For holiday entertaining, double or triple the recipe and place in a pot or Crock-Pot to keep warm. Drop in a fresh cinnamon stick and a few twists of fresh orange peel as garnishes.

Creamy Iced Coffee

It's amazing how popular coffee drinks have become. Many of my clients use them as an afternoon pick-me-up. The only problem is that these drinks are loaded with calories and sugar. In fact, a small coffeehouse drink often contains more sugar than a can of cola. Quick and easy to make this version has a fraction of the calories (and cost!). The trick to getting a silky texture without sugar is to use non-fat half-and-half in place of milk.

- 1/2 **cup double strength coffee**
  or 2 tsp instant coffee dissolved in 4 ounces of warm water
  (regular or decaffeinated)
- 1/4 **cup non-fat half-and-half**
- 2 **Tbs Splenda**
- 1/2 **cup crushed ice**

Pour the coffee, half-and-half, and the Splenda into a blender. Blend to mix. Add the ice and blend briefly (about 15 seconds) until ice is incorporated but pieces still remain. Pour into an 8-ounce glass. *One serving.*

Per serving:

Calories 48
Carbohydrate 8 grams (sugar 4)
Protein 2 grams
Diabetic exchange = 1/2 carbohydrate

Fat 0.5 grams (saturated 0)
Fiber 0 grams
Sodium 60 milligrams

A 9.5-ounce bottle of Starbuck's
Frappucino contains 31 grams of sugar.

Frosty Mocha

A delicious twist on the original. In addition to the chocolate, I've added more ice to make this 12-ounce version tall and frosty. Don't forget to have a straw ready!

½ cup double-strength coffee or 2 tsp instant
    coffee dissolved in 4 ounces of warm water
    (regular or decaffeinated)
¼ cup + 1 Tbs non-fat half-and-half
3 Tbs Splenda
1 tsp unsweetened cocoa powder
1 cup crushed ice

Pour the coffee, half-and-half, Splenda, and cocoa powder into a blender. Blend to mix. Add half of the ice and blend briefly (about 15 seconds) until ice is incorporated. Add the rest of the ice and blend once more. Pour into a tall 12-ounce glass. *One serving.*

Per serving:

Calories 61
Carbohydrate 10 (sugar 5)
Protein 2 grams
Diabetic exchange = ½ carbohydrate

Fat 0.5 gram (saturated 0)
Fiber 0 grams
Sodium 67 milligrams

The good news about Au Bon Pain's Frozen Mocha Blast
(16 ounces) is that it has only 3 grams of fat. The bad news
is that at 320 calories, it contains over 60 grams of sugar.

Strawberry Banana Smoothie

Whether you like your smoothies thick and creamy or cool and frosty, this recipe fits the bill. Great for a snack or as part of a meal, this drink is loaded with calcium and vitamin C, but not with the usual sugar and fat. It also makes use of those overripe bananas—simply peel them and place them in a plastic bag before freezing. Frozen bananas will keep for a month or more.

1	cup 1% (or skim) milk
1	cup plain, non-fat yogurt
1	cup sliced strawberries (about eight medium)
2	Tbs Splenda
½	large banana (frozen)

Thick and creamy: Place milk into a blender. Add yogurt, strawberries, and Splenda. Pulse. Add the banana and blend until thick and creamy.

Cool and Frosty: Add 1 additional tablespoon of Splenda and ½ cup crushed ice to the thick and creamy smoothie. Blend on high for 30 seconds longer until ice is incorporated. *Two servings.*

Per serving:

Calories 150
Carbohydrate 24 grams (sugar 20)
Protein 10 grams
Diabetic exchange = 1 low-fat milk, ½ fruit

Fat 2 grams (saturated 1)
Fiber 2 grams
Sodium 65 milligrams

Add a scoop of protein powder to make a tasty high-protein shake or enjoy with a handful of low-fat wheat crackers and a tablespoon of peanut butter for a wholesome low-calorie mini-meal.

Berry Blast Smoothie

I recently saw a drink similar to this in a magazine touting its anti-cancer properties. Berries are full of compounds that are powerful foes to tumors, but I love this drink because it is so delicious. Any combination of berries will do—just make sure one type is frozen.

- ½ cup 1% (or skim) milk
- 1 cup plain non-fat yogurt
- ½ cup blueberries
- ½ cup frozen strawberries
- ¼ cup Splenda
- 1 cup crushed (or cubed) ice

Place milk into a blender. Add remaining ingredients. Pulse. Add ice and bend at high speed until smooth. *Two Servings.*

Per serving:

Calories 150
Carbohydrate 23 grams (sugar 18)
Protein 9 grams
Diabetic exchange = 1 low-fat milk, ½ fruit

Fat 2.5 grams (saturated 1.5)
Fiber 2 grams
Sodium 145 milligrams

Orange Sunshine Smoothie

*R*eminiscent of a creamsicle, this is a wonderful addition to any breakfast. *This creamy drink still delivers a full day's worth of vitamin C with less sugar and more protein than a cup of plain orange juice.*

- ½ **cup orange juice**
- ¼ **cup plain non-fat yogurt**
- ½ **cup crushed (or cubed) ice**
- I **Tbs Splenda**

Place all ingredients into a blender. Blend at high speed for 30 to 45 seconds. *One serving.*

Per serving:

Calories 100
Carbohydrate 19 grams (sugar 17)
Protein 5 grams
Diabetic exchange = 1 fruit, ½ non-fat milk

Fat 0 grams
Fiber 0 grams
Sodium 145 milligrams

Muffins, Coffeecakes, and Breakfast Breads

*L*et's face it—we all love to have a sweet treat to start the day. Muffins, coffeecakes, and sweet breads give us a legitimate excuse to do so. Unfortunately, most of them are simply filled with sugar and fat, which, of course translates into lots of calories. Because I also have a sweet tooth in the morning, I have taught classes and developed recipes to bring down the fat in these morning favorites. But when it came to reducing the sugar, things got tough. I remember making muffins for a group of children with diabetes and no matter how I tried, I had to use more sugar than I would have liked to get a good quality, sweet tasting muffin.

I am now pleased to report that you can now have these treats—without the extra fat and tons of sugar—whenever you'd like. These were some of the first recipes I created and I can tell you my testers were amazed when they were told how low in calories, fat, and sugar these items are. Why? Because they taste wonderful!

Apple Oatmeal Streusel Muffins
Best Bran Muffins
Blueberry Muffins
Cranberry Orange Muffins
Sour Cream Chocolate Chocolate Chip Muffins
Quick Cake with Coconut and Almonds
Gingerbread Coffeecake
Raspberry Almond Tea Cake
Blueberry Buckle Cake
Cinnamon Streusel Coffeecake
Pumpkin Pecan Bread with Orange Cream Cheese
Wholesome Banana Bread

Mega Muffin Mania

Somewhere along the line, something happened to the average size muffin—it's been replaced by super-size wonders just about everywhere! Not to say these monstrous muffins don't have appeal, obviously they do. It's just that instead of a snack or a quick breakfast bite they've turned into full meals, only many people don't realize it.

Food labeling laws state a serving of a muffin to be 2 ounces, but today's mega-muffins average 4 to 6 ounces. If you read the label carefully, you'll find your muffin may technically be considered three servings. This means if you multiply by 3 all the numbers on the nutritional analysis label, you now have the real facts on these muffins that weigh in at 500 to 600 calories, with 18 to 24 grams of fat and as much as 90 grams of carbohydrate (that's six bread servings—ouch!).

The muffins here are made in traditional 2½ inch muffin tins (cupcake size). They are equivalent to a 2½ to 3-ounce muffin (baked goods with Splenda weigh less than usual). If you want to splurge, you can bake them in the large tins 3 inches wide and bake them 4 to 5 minutes longer. The recipes will make half as many and you can simply double the nutrition information. With these healthy muffins, you can afford to.

Muffin Comparison*

Muffins	Calories	Fat (grams)	Carbohydrate (grams)	Sugar (grams)
Regular Mega Muffin (6 oz.)	540	24	72	42
Low-Fat Mega Muffin	480	9	94	54
No Added Sugar Mega Muffin	390	16	60	3
Splenda Mega Muffin	290	8	44	4
Splenda 2½ oz. Muffin	145	4	22	2

*Nutrient information from BJ's Warehouse Club and the average nutritional content of Splenda muffin recipes in this book

Apple Oatmeal Streusel Muffins

These are so good and good for you. These hearty muffins made with fresh apple, oats, and whole wheat flour are a great way to start the day!

MUFFIN BATTER

1 cup all-purpose flour	1 large egg
1 cup whole wheat flour	1 large egg white
2 tsp baking powder	1/2 cup low-fat buttermilk
1/2 tsp baking soda	1/2 cup unsweetened
1/2 tsp cream of tartar	applesauce
2 tsp cinnamon	2 Tbs canola oil
1/2 tsp nutmeg	3/4 cup Splenda Granular
1/4 tsp salt	1 cup peeled, grated cooking apple

STREUSEL TOPPING

2 Tbs all-purpose flour	1 Tbs brown sugar
4 Tbs uncooked oatmeal (not instant)	(optional)
	1/2 tsp cinnamon
2 Tbs Splenda Granular	2 tsp margarine

Preheat oven to 375 degrees. Spray 12 muffin cups or liners with non-stick cooking spray.

To make streusel topping—place all of the streusel ingredients in a small bowl except margarine and stir until thoroughly mixed. Cut in margarine until crumbly. Set aside. Measure flour, baking powder, baking soda, cream of tartar, cinnamon, nutmeg, and salt into a large bowl. Stir to mix. In a separate bowl, beat the egg and egg white with the buttermilk until foamy. Into this mixture, stir in the applesauce, oil, Splenda, and the grated apple. Make a well in the center of the flour mixture and pour in the apple mixture. Stir just until moistened. Do not overmix. Spoon batter into prepared muffin tins, filling 2/3 full. Top each muffin with streusel. Bake for 15 minutes or until a toothpick comes out clean when placed into the center of the muffin. Remove from baking tins and cool on wire racks. *Twelve servings.*

Per serving:

Calories 155	Fat 5 grams (saturated 0.5)
Carbohydrate 23 grams (sugar 3)	Fiber 2 grams
Protein 4 grams	Sodium 200 milligrams
Diabetic exchange = 1 1/2 carbohydrate, 1 fat	

A 1.3-ounce Snackwell's apple breakfast bar has 17 grams of sugar (29 carbohydrate grams total).

Best Bran Muffins

While everyone assumes bran muffins are good for you, most of them are chock full of sugar and fat. Bursting with flavor, these dark and moist muffins are a good source of fiber, vitamin C, and iron, without the stuff you don't want (or need). My husband is my expert bran muffin taster and has officially requested I make a lot more of these!

2 large egg whites	½ cup whole wheat flour
I cup low-fat buttermilk	½ cup Splenda Granular
1½ cups 100% bran cereal (not flakes)	I tsp baking soda
3 Tbs molasses	1½ tsp baking powder
2 Tbs canola oil	½ tsp cream of tartar
I tsp finely grated orange peel	¼ cup finely chopped dried
½ cup all-purpose flour	cranberries, raisins, or nuts*

Preheat oven to 375 degrees. Spray 8 muffin cups or liners in muffin tins with nonstick cooking spray. In a medium bowl, whip the egg whites and buttermilk until frothy. Add the bran cereal, molasses, oil, orange peel, and cranberries if desired and set aside for 5 minutes.

Measure flours, Splenda, baking soda, baking powder, and cream of tartar into a large bowl. Stir to mix. Make a well in the center of the dry ingredients and pour in the bran mixture. Using a large spoon or spatula stir just until all the flour is moistened. Spoon batter into muffin cups filling ¾ full. Bake for 18 minutes or until a toothpick when placed into the center of the muffin comes out clean. Cool in pan for 5 minutes. Remove and place on wire rack to cool. Store in an airtight container. *Eight servings.*

Per serving:

Calories 160
Carbohydrate 29 grams (sugar 10)
Protein 5 grams
Diabetic exchange = 1½ bread, ½ fat

Fat 4.5 grams (saturated 0.5)
Fiber 5 grams
Sodium 325 milligrams

* For dried fruit, add 3 grams of carbohydrate and 12 calories per serving. For nuts add 0.5 grams carbohydrate, 2 grams fat, and 24 calories per serving.

> Foods high in fiber have been shown to have a positive effect on maintaining blood sugar levels. The recommended guideline for fiber intake is 25 grams or more per day.

Blueberry Muffins

*T*he most popular muffin? Why, blueberry, of course. These moist low-fat muffins are a breeze to make and a joy to eat. These can be made with frozen berries but are an extra special treat when fresh blueberries are available. The lemon yogurt helps to keep them moist and adds a nice flavor.

2   cups all-purpose flour
1   Tbs baking powder
½   tsp baking soda
1   cup blueberries (do not thaw if frozen)
1   tsp finely grated lemon peel
1   large egg
3   Tbs canola oil
½   cup Splenda Granular
1   8-oz cup low-fat lemon yogurt
6   Tbs 1% milk
1½ tsp vanilla
1   tsp sugar (optional)

Preheat oven to 375 degrees. Spray 12 muffin cups or liners in muffin tins with nonstick cooking spray. Measure flour, baking powder, and baking soda into a large bowl. Stir with a whisk. Add blueberries and lemon peel. Set aside.

In a small bowl, whisk egg until frothy. Add oil, Splenda, yogurt, milk, and vanilla. Whisk until smooth. Make a well in the dry ingredients and pour in the yogurt mixture. Using a large spoon or spatula, stir just until all the flour is moistened. Do not overmix the muffin batter. Spoon batter into muffin cups filling ⅔ full. If desired, measure out ½ teaspoon of sugar and sprinkle lightly over 6 muffins. Repeat. Bake for 18 to 20 minutes, or until a toothpick comes out clean when placed into the center of the muffin. Remove and place on wire rack to cool. *Twelve servings.*

Per serving:

Calories 145
Carbohydrate 23 grams (sugar 6)
Protein 4 grams
Diabetic exchange = 1½ carbohydrate, ½ fat

Fat 4.5 grams (saturated 0.5)
Fiber 0.5 grams
Sodium 200 milligrams

> Do not substitute "light" or low-calorie lemon yogurt. The sugar in the regular low-fat yogurt helps the muffin sides and bottoms brown. Remember, each muffin has only 1/12 cup of sweetened yogurt in it!

Cranberry Orange Muffins

The classic combination of orange and cranberries has become one of the most popular for muffins. The orange juice imparts a sweet and bold flavor and is a perfect complement to the tart cranberries. While these are great during the holidays when cranberries are in season, you can enjoy them year-round by throwing a few bags of cranberries in your freezer or substituting blueberries in the summer.

2	cups all-purpose flour	½	cup orange juice
2	tsp baking powder	½	cup 1% or skim milk
½	tsp baking soda	1	cup Splenda Granular
¼	tsp salt	1	Tbs orange zest
1¼	cups fresh cranberries	¼	cup orange juice
1	large egg	2	Tbs Splenda Granular
¼	cup canola oil	1	Tbs reduced sugar orange marmalade (optional)

Preheat oven to 375 degrees. Spray 12 muffin cups or liners in muffin tins with nonstick cooking spray.

Measure flour, baking powder, soda, salt, and cranberries into a large bowl and stir. Set aside. In a small bowl whisk the egg, oil, orange juice, milk, Splenda, and zest together. Make a well in the center of the dry ingredients and pour in the milk mixture. Using a large spoon or spatula, mix just until all the flour is moistened. Do not overmix. Spoon into the prepared muffin tins, filling ⅔ full. Bake for 20 minutes or until a toothpick comes out clean when placed into the center of the muffin. While muffins are baking, place the ¼ cup orange juice and 2 tablespoons of Splenda (and marmalade) into a small pot or microwaveable bowl. Heat gently until mixture reduces by one half. Remove muffins from the oven and brush each muffin with the orange mixture. Remove muffins from tins and place on rack to cool. *Twelve servings.*

Per serving:

Calories 150
Carbohydrate 22 grams (sugar 3)
Protein 3 grams
Diabetic exchange = 1½ carbohydrate, 1 fat

Fat 5 grams (saturated 0.5)
Fiber 1 gram
Sodium 250 milligrams

> Watch for "no sugar added" cranberry juice. It contains 32 grams of added sugar in the form of fruit juice concentrates.

Sour Cream Chocolate Chocolate Chip Muffins

I must admit just seeing the word chocolate twice in the title is enough to make me take notice. This is "dessert for breakfast" at its best. These light-textured muffins are so rich with chocolate they could be used in place of cupcakes. My kids and their friends adore them as an after school snack with a cold glass of milk.

1½ cups all-purpose flour	2 egg whites
⅓ cup Dutch-process cocoa powder (like Hershey's European)	3 Tbs canola oil
	½ cup unsweetened applesauce
1½ tsp baking powder	⅔ cup 1% or skim milk
½ tsp baking soda	¼ cup light or nonfat sour cream
⅓ cup mini semisweet chocolate chips	1 cup Splenda Granular
	1 tsp vanilla
2 Tbs brown sugar	2 tsp powdered sugar (optional)

Preheat oven to 375 degrees. Spray 10 muffin tins or liners in muffin tins with nonstick cooking spray. Sift flour, cocoa powder, baking powder, and baking soda into a large bowl. Stir in chocolate chips. Add brown sugar. Set aside. In a medium bowl, beat the egg whites until frothy. Add the oil, applesauce, milk, sour cream, Splenda, and vanilla and whisk until smooth. Make a well in the center of the dry ingredients and pour in the liquid mixture. Using a large spoon or spatula, mix just until all the flour is moistened. Do not overmix. Spoon into prepared muffin tins, filling ⅔ full. Bake for 15 to 18 minutes or until a toothpick comes out clean when placed into the center of the muffin. (The muffin tops will have a dull finish.) Remove muffins from oven. Use a small sifter or mesh strainer to sprinkle powdered sugar over tops of muffins if desired. *Ten servings.*

Per serving:

Calories 160
Carbohydrate 24 grams (sugar 7)
Protein 4 grams
Diabetic exchange = 1½ carbohydrate, 1 fat

Fat 7 grams (saturated 1.5)
Fiber 2 grams
Sodium 190 milligrams

> Using cocoa powder and mini chocolate chips (they disperse better so you can use less) are two ways to incorporate the great flavor of chocolate into low-fat recipes.

Quick Cake with Coconut and Almonds

This coffeecake really is quick! Light and tender, it takes advantage of the new low-fat baking mixes. The cake is mixed in one bowl and then topped with a yummy mixture of coconut and almonds before baking. Just add a Sunday morning paper and a cup of coffee and you're all set.

1½	cups reduced fat baking mix (like Reduced Fat Bisquick)
½	cup Splenda Granular
½	tsp baking powder
⅔	cup 1% or skim milk
1	large egg
1	Tbs canola oil
½	tsp vanilla
6	Tbs shredded coconut
2	Tbs Splenda Granular
1	Tbs brown sugar
3	Tbs sliced almonds
1	Tbs melted margarine

Preheat oven to 350 degrees. Spray an 8-inch square baking pan with nonstick cooking spray.

Measure the baking mix, ½ cup Splenda and baking powder into a large mixing bowl. Add the milk, egg, oil, and vanilla. Stir just until smooth. Spoon into prepared pan. Place the coconut, 2 tablespoons Splenda, brown sugar, and almonds in a small bowl. Add the margarine and mix. Sprinkle this mixture over the top of the cake. Bake for 20 minutes or until the center springs back when gently touched. *Nine servings.*

Per serving:

Calories 160
Carbohydrate 20 grams (sugar 5)
Protein 3 grams
Diabetic exchange = 1½ carbohydrate, 1 fat

Fat 7 grams (saturated 2)
Fiber 1 gram
Sodium 270 milligrams

Switching to low-fat baking mixes is an easy way to cut back on unnecessary fat.

Gingerbread Coffeecake

*T*his tender and very light-textured cake may become your next Christmas classic. Not overly sweet, but with a subtle taste of gingerbread, it would make a fine treat after a hard day of holiday shopping.

I	cup all-purpose flour	1/2	tsp baking soda
1/2	cup Splenda Granular	1/2	cup low fat buttermilk
3/4	tsp cinnamon	I	Tbs + 2 tsp molasses
3/4	tsp ginger	I	large egg
1/4	tsp allspice	I	Tbs Splenda Granular
4	Tbs margarine	I	tsp cinnamon
3/4	tsp baking powder		

Preheat oven to 350 degrees. Spray an 8-inch round cake pan with non-stick cooking spray. Stir flour and lightly measure 1 cup. Combine flour, 1/2 cup Splenda, and spices in a large bowl. Cut in the margarine using a pastry blender or fork until the mixture resembles small crumbs. Measure out 1/3 cup and set aside.

To the large bowl of flour, add the baking powder, baking soda, buttermilk, molasses, and egg. Beat with a spoon or on low speed with a mixer until smooth. Spoon into the prepared pan. Add the tablespoon of Splenda and teaspoon of cinnamon to the reserved crumb mixture. Sprinkle mixture over the top of the cake. Bake for 25 minutes or until the center of the cake springs back when touched lightly. *Eight servings.*

Per serving

Calories 130
Carbohydrate 17 grams (sugar 3)
Protein 3 grams
Diabetic exchange = I carbohydrate, I fat

Fat 6 grams (saturated 1.5)
Fiber 0.5 grams
Sodium 200 milligrams

Watch out for that cinnamon roll at the mall. They weigh in at almost 700 calories with 34 grams of fat and over 80 grams of carbohydrate. That's more than eating half this cake all by yourself.

Raspberry Almond Tea Cake

This cake is picture perfect. Inspired by Cooking Light *magazine I retooled this delightful crumb cake. Splenda helped me to lower the sugar to only 3 grams. Make it when you can get fresh raspberries and have a little extra time to put it together. This coffeecake is definitely worth it.*

1	cup all-purpose flour		1	tsp vanilla
1/2	cup Splenda Granular		1/2	tsp almond extract
4	Tbs margarine		1/4	cup low-fat cottage cheese
2	Tbs sliced almonds		2	Tbs light tub cream cheese
2	egg whites		1	Tbs + 1 tsp Splenda Granular
1	tsp baking powder		1/4	cup low sugar-raspberry preserves
3/4	tsp baking soda		1/2	cup fresh raspberries
2	Tbs 1% or skim milk			

Preheat oven to 350 degrees. Spray an 8-inch round spring-form or cake pan with nonstick cooking spray. Stir flour and lightly measure 1 cup. Combine flour and 1/2 cup Splenda in a large bowl. Cut in the margarine using a pastry blender or fork until the mixture resembles small crumbs. Measure out 6 tablespoons into a small bowl, add almonds, and set aside.

Place the egg whites into a bowl and beat until soft peaks form. Set aside.

To the large bowl of crumbs, add the baking powder and soda, milk, and extracts. Use mixer on low speed and beat until blended. Fold in the beaten egg whites with a spatula or spoon and spoon batter into prepared pan.

Purée cottage cheese until smooth, add cream cheese and remaining Splenda and pulse again until thick and creamy. Spread evenly over the cake batter. Dot the cheese mixture with the preserves and top with the raspberries.

Sprinkle almond crumb mixture over entire cake. Bake for 20 minutes or until cake springs back when touched lightly in the center. *Eight servings.*

Per serving:

Calories 140
Carbohydrate 17 grams (sugar 3)
Protein 4 grams
Diabetic exchange = 1 carbohydrate, 1 fat

Fat 6 grams (saturated 1.5)
Fiber 1 gram
Sodium 230 milligrams

Blueberry Buckle Cake

*T*his is the perfect coffeecake for your next brunch. Bursting with blueberries, it's topped with a streusel flecked with orange rind and just a touch of sugar for a glistening appearance. Make it in the height of summer when blueberries are in season. Your guests will surely thank you.

1½ cups all-purpose flour	¾ cup low-fat buttermilk
1½ tsp baking powder	⅓ cup all-purpose flour
½ tsp baking soda	¼ cup Splenda Granular
½ cup Splenda Granular	1 tsp orange rind
1 cup blueberries (½ pint)	3 Tbs light butter, chilled
2 Tbs canola oil	2 tsp granulated sugar
1 large egg	(optional)

Preheat oven to 350 degrees. Spray an 8-inch square baking pan with nonstick cooking spray. Sift 1½ cups flour, baking powder, and baking soda into a large bowl. Stir. Add ½ cup Splenda and blueberries. In a small bowl whisk the oil, egg, and buttermilk. Make a well in the center of the dry ingredients and pour in the buttermilk mixture. Stir briefly just to combine. Spoon into the prepared pan and smooth the top.

In another small bowl, place ⅓ cup flour, ¼ cup Splenda, and orange rind. Cut in the light butter until mixture resembles small crumbs. Sprinkle over the top of the cake. Measure sugar and sprinkle over entire top of cake. Bake for 20 to 23 minutes or until a toothpick comes out clean when placed in the center. Do not overbake. *Nine servings.*

Per serving:

Calories 160
Carbohydrate 26 grams (sugar 4)
Protein 4 grams
Diabetic exchange = 1½ carbohydrate, 1 fat

Fat 4.5 grams (saturated 1)
Fiber 2 grams
Sodium 190 milligrams

> Just a touch of sugar, when spread on top, goes a long way and only adds one gram of carbohydrate per piece.

Cinnamon Streusel Coffeecake

This is the granddaddy of all coffeecakes. I don't know anyone who hasn't seen, eaten, or made a coffeecake like this. With its streusel in the middle and on top, it's no wonder it's a favorite. It usually starts out with a stick of butter—or two—add some sour cream, a lot of sugar, nuts, whew! I knew I had my work cut out for me here.

It took a few tries, but I finally came up with the big, showy cake I was looking for. Be sure to wrap up the cake to seal in the moisture after you cut into it. The lower fat content will cause it to dry out faster.

CAKE
- 3 cups cake flour
- 1 Tbs baking powder
- 3/4 tsp baking soda
- 1/3 cup margarine
- 1 large egg
- 1 1/3 cups Splenda Granular
- 4 large egg whites
- 1/2 cup unsweetened applesauce
- 2 tsp vanilla
- 1 1/2 cups light sour cream

STREUSEL
- 2/3 cup graham cracker crumbs
- 2/3 cup Splenda Granular
- 1/3 cup chopped nuts
- 2 Tbs cinnamon
- 1 Tbs canola oil
- 1 Tbs brown sugar

Preheat oven to 350 degrees. Spray a 10-inch tube pan (angel food pan) or nonstick bundt pan with nonstick cooking spray.

Combine the streusel ingredients except the oil and brown sugar in a bowl and set aside.

Sift the cake flour, baking powder, and soda into a medium bowl.

In a large mixing bowl, cream the margarine with an electric mixer. Add the Splenda and then the egg and continue to beat until smooth. Add the egg whites and vanilla. Beat briefly to incorporate. Beat in the applesauce. Add the sifted flour mixture and beat at medium speed just until smooth. Add the sour cream and blend just until incorporated and batter is uniform. Spoon half of batter into the bottom of the prepared pan. Spread with a spoon to smooth. Sprinkle half of the streusel mixture over the batter. Drop the remaining batter by spoonfuls over the streusel and carefully spread. Using the back of a spoon coated with cooking spray will help. Add the oil and brown sugar to the remaining streusel. Sprinkle on top. Bake for 35 to 40 minutes or until a toothpick inserted near the center comes out clean. Let cool, in pan, on rack. To serve, lift out of pan and remove cake from center cone. *Sixteen servings.*

Per serving:

Calories 195
Carbohydrate 24 grams (sugar 5)
Protein 5 grams
Diabetic exchange = 1½ carbohydrate, 1½ fat

Fat 8.5 grams (saturated 3)
Fiber 1 gram
Sodium 250 milligrams

Pumpkin Pecan Bread
with Orange Cream Cheese

This holiday favorite is sure to please the most discerning of your guests. Serve it with the Orange Cream Cheese on page 134 for a delicious taste treat.

1/4 cup canola oil	1 3/4 cup all-purpose flour
1 cup pumpkin purée	1 tsp baking powder
1 large egg	1/2 tsp baking soda
1 large egg white	1 1/2 tsp cinnamon
1/2 cup low-fat buttermilk	1/2 tsp ginger
2 Tbs molasses	1/4 tsp cloves
1 cup + 2 Tbs Splenda Granular	1/3 cup chopped pecans

Orange Cream Cheese, page 134

Preheat oven to 350 F. Coat a 9 × 5-inch loaf pan with nonstick cooking spray. In a medium bowl, whisk together the oil, pumpkin, whole egg, egg white, buttermilk, molasses, and Splenda. In a large bowl, measure the flour, baking powder, baking soda, spices, and nuts. Stir and make a well in the center of the dry ingredients. Pour the pumpkin mixture into the well and stir just until all flour is moistened. Do not overmix. Spoon the batter into the prepared pan and bake for 40 minutes until the crack appears dry and a toothpick placed into the center of the bread comes out clean. Allow the bread to cool in the pan for 10 minutes. Remove the loaf from pan and set back on rack to finish cooling. Slice and serve with Orange Cream Cheese if desired. *Twelve servings.*

Per serving:

Calories 170	Fat 7 grams (saturated 0.5)
Carbohydrate 22 grams (sugar 4)	Fiber 1 gram
Protein 4 grams	Sodium 170 milligrams
Diabetic exchange = 1 1/2 carbohydrate, 1 fat	

Did you know that a large bagel can have up to 70 grams of carbohydrate?

Wholesome Banana Bread

This banana bread is incredibly sweet, dense, and moist. It is sturdy enough to pack and would make a great addition to anyone's lunch.

1 cup all-purpose white flour	1/4 cup low-fat buttermilk
1/2 cup whole wheat flour	4 Tbs margarine
1 tsp baking soda	2 Tbs prune purée
1/2 tsp baking powder	1 1/2 tsp vanilla
1 1/3 cups mashed ripe bananas (about 3 medium whole ripe bananas)	3/4 cup Splenda Granular
	1 egg

Preheat oven to 350 degrees. Spray one 9 × 5-inch loaf pan or two 6 × 3½-inch mini-loaves with nonstick cooking spray.

Sift together flours, baking soda and powder. Set aside. Mash the bananas in a small bowl and stir in the buttermilk; mix and set aside. In a large bowl, cream the margarine with an electric mixer on medium speed. Add the prune purée and beat well. Beat in the vanilla and the Splenda. Add the egg. On low speed, alternate adding the banana mixture and the flour mixture, adding half of the flour and mixing until just incorporated and then half the banana. Repeat once.

Turn mixture into prepared pan(s) and smooth top. Bake for 40 to 45 minutes for a 9 × 5 pan and 30 to 35 minutes for 2 mini-loaves until a cake tester inserted into the middle of the loaf comes out dry. Let cool in pan for twenty minutes on cooling rack. Remove loaf from pan and set back on rack to finish cooling. Can keep for several days. Wrap well. *Twelve servings.*

Per serving:

Calories 130
Carbohydrate 21 grams (sugar 6)
Protein 3 grams
Diabetic exchange = 1 carbohydrate; 1/2 fruit, 1 fat

Fat 4 grams (saturated 1)
Fiber 2 grams
Sodium 170 milligrams

Fruit purées are great for adding moistness to quick breads without fat. Bananas have the additional benefit of being a great source of potassium.

For the Love
of Cookies

I've been baking cookies for as long as I can remember (I literally started as a child). Now I bake cookies with my kids. There are a lot of reasons I love baking cookies. Cookies are fun. Cookies are easy. Cookies can be tasted as soon as they are made! When I think of whipping up quick treats that are great to share, cookies are the answer. Yet, as I thought of creating winning baked goods that would be low in fat and sugar, cookies did not jump to the forefront. The truth is that most low-fat cookies are made with extra sugar to compensate for the reduction in fat. Sugar performs many functions in cookies in addition to making them sweet. Sugar also helps cookies to spread and makes them tender, brown, and crisp. In some cakey bar cookies, these attributes are not as important, but in standard drop cookies, these are the very qualities that make a cookie a cookie! Thus, you will find small amounts of sugar in all the drop cookies. Remember, when it comes to good health and good cooking, it's not about all or nothing, but balance. I have reduced the amount of added sugar in these low-fat cookies by 75 percent (or more), so instead of adding it by the cupful you add it by the spoonful. The result is a cookie that can compete with its full sugar and fat rivals. They look and taste wonderful (just ask my two cookie-gobbling kids), and can be enjoyed by everyone. Bake a batch and let the fun begin!

Chocolate Chip Cookies
Great Oatmeal Cookies
Peanut Butter Cookies
Chocolate Chocolate Chip Cookies
Creamy Lemon Bars
Apricot Oatmeal Bars
Frosted Pumpkin Bars
Raspberry Shortbread Triangles

Chocolate Chip Cookies

These chocolate chip cookies look and taste like the real McCoy. There are slightly soft, sweet, and full of chocolate. One of my tasters said it this way, "they're perfect." I've reduced the sugar by 75 percent and the fat by one-half, compared to the traditional recipe. But more importantly, no one will ever know.

I	cup all-purpose flour	3	Tbs brown sugar
½	tsp baking soda	I	large egg white
¼	cup margarine, softened	I½	tsp vanilla
2	Tbs prune purée	6	Tbs mini chocolate chips
⅔	cup Splenda Granular		

Preheat oven to 375 degrees. Spray cookie sheet with nonstick cooking spray.

Combine flour and baking soda together in a small bowl. Set aside. In a medium mixing bowl, with an electric mixer, beat margarine, prune purée, Splenda, and brown sugar until creamy. Add egg white and vanilla. Beat well. Stir in the flour mixture. Stir in chocolate chips. Drop dough, by level table-spoons, onto cookie sheet. Press down on dough with the bottom of a glass or spatula to flatten. Bake cookies for 4 minutes or until they "puff." Open oven and tap cookie sheet firmly against baking rack or the inside of the oven door to force cookies to drop and spread slightly. Place cookies back in oven and bake 5 more minutes, or until lightly browned. Remove from pan and cool on rack. Cookies will remain crisp for several hours, then soften.

Variation: Replace the prune purée with and additional 2 tablespoons of margarine. Calories per cookie will increase by 5, and fat grams by 1. Both the carbohydrate and sugar content will be reduced by 1 gram. *Eighteen servings.*

Per serving:

Calories 80	Fat 3.5 grams (saturated 1)
Carbohydrate 11.5 grams (sugar 5)	Fiber 0.5 grams
Protein 1 grams	Sodium 60 milligrams

Diabetic exchange = 1 carbohydrate, ½ fat (2 cookies = 1½ carbohydrate, 1 fat)

If you substitute 1 tablespoon of corn syrup for 1 of the tablespoons of brown sugar, the outside of the cookie will stay crisper. You will still be averaging a mere 1 teaspoon of sugar per cookie.

Great Oatmeal Cookies

*A*nother classic cookie jar recipe. Many low-fat oatmeal cookie recipes replace some, or all of the fat, with applesauce. I found that doing so, in conjunction with the significant reduction in sugar, produced a very gummy cookie. My cookie uses butter for flavor, oil for tenderness, and prune purée for color and texture. The result is a low-fat, low-sugar cookie that is worthy of the cookie jar.

¾ cup all-purpose flour	⅔ cup Splenda Granular
1½ cups dry oatmeal (not instant)	3 Tbs brown sugar
½ tsp baking soda	1 large egg
1 tsp cinnamon	1 tsp vanilla
2 Tbs butter, softened	¼ cup dried cranberries,
2 Tbs canola oil	finely chopped
2 Tbs prune purée	½ tsp grated orange zest

Preheat oven to 350 degrees. Spray cookie sheet with nonstick cooking spray.

Combine flour, oatmeal, baking soda, and cinnamon together in a bowl. Set aside.

In a medium mixing bowl, with an electric mixer, beat butter, oil, prune purée, Splenda, and brown sugar until creamy. Add egg and vanilla. Beat well. Stir in cranberries and zest and then flour mixture. Drop dough, by level tablespoons, onto cookie sheet. Press down on dough with the bottom of a glass to flatten. Bake cookies for 4 minutes or until they "puff." Open oven and tap cookie sheet firmly against baking rack or the inside of the oven door to force cookies to drop and spread slightly. Place cookies back in oven and bake 5 to 7 more minutes, or until lightly browned.

Remove from pan and cool on rack. (Cookies will remain crisp for several hours, then soften. *Twenty-two servings.*

Per serving:

Calories 75
Carbohydrate 11 grams (sugar 3.5)
Protein 2 grams
Diabetic exchange = 1 carbohydrate, ½ fat (2 cookies = 1½ carbohydrate, 1 fat)

Fat 3 grams (saturated 1)
Fiber 0.5 grams
Sodium 35 milligrams

To make old-fashioned oatmeal raisin cookies, substitute raisins for the dried cranberries, eliminate the orange zest, and increase the vanilla and cinnamon by ½ teaspoon each.

Peanut Butter Cookies

Some of my most enjoyable cooking classes have been with children. My goal in selecting a recipe is to choose foods kids love, in order to teach them the importance of good nutrition. These cookies have been a great tool because they provide a healthy alternative to junk food and kids love them.

1½	cups all-purpose flour	¾	cup Splenda Granular
1	tsp baking soda	3	Tbs brown sugar
½	tsp baking powder	1	large egg
½	cup + 2 Tbs peanut butter	2	Tbs 1% milk
¼	cup margarine	2	tsp vanilla
2	Tbs non-fat cream cheese		

Preheat oven to 375 degrees. Spray cookie sheet with nonstick cooking spray.

Combine flour, baking soda, and baking powder together in a bowl. Set aside. In a medium mixing bowl, with an electric mixer, beat peanut butter, margarine, cream cheese, Splenda, and brown sugar until creamy. Add egg, milk, and vanilla. Beat well. Stir in flour mixture. Roll dough, by level tablespoon, into balls. Place onto cookie sheet and flatten with a fork forming a criss-cross on top of each cookie. Bake for 9 to 10 minutes. Remove from pan and cool on rack. *Twenty-six servings.*

Per serving:

Calories 90
Carbohydrate 8.5 grams (sugar 3)
Protein 3 grams
Diabetic exchange = ½ carbohydrate, 1 fat

Fat 5 grams (saturated 1)
Fiber 0.5 grams
Sodium 45 milligrams

These make the perfect balanced after-school snack—fun to eat and filled with protein and "healthy" fat for energy. Round out this snack with a nice cool glass of low-fat milk.

Chocolate Chocolate Chip Cookies

Chocolate and more chocolate—my kids thought these were the best. These are soft, and oh-so-full of chocolate. The added milk helps them to spread nicely with a only a touch of sugar.

1	cup all-purpose flour	1/2	cup Splenda Granular
3	Tbs Dutch-process cocoa powder	3	Tbs brown sugar
	(like Hershey's European)	1	egg
1/2	tsp baking soda	1	tsp vanilla
1/3	cup 70% vegetable oil margarine	2	Tbs 1% milk
2	Tbs prune purée	1/3	cup mini chocolate chips

Preheat oven to 375 degrees. Spray cookie sheet with nonstick cooking spray.

Combine flour, cocoa, and baking soda together in a small bowl. Set aside. In a medium mixing bowl, with an electric mixer, beat margarine; prune purée, Splenda, and brown sugar until creamy. Add egg and vanilla. Beat well. Stir in the flour mixture, alternating with milk. Stir in chocolate chips. Drop dough, by level tablespoons, onto cookie sheet. Press down on dough with the bottom of a glass to flatten. Bake cookies for 8 to 10 minutes. Remove from pan and cool on rack. *Twenty-four servings.*

Per serving:

Calories 60
Carbohydrate 8 grams (sugar 3)
Protein 1 gram
Diabetic exchange = 1/2 carbohydrate, 1/2 fat

Fat 3 grams (saturated 1)
Fiber 0.5 grams
Sodium 30 milligrams

Good news—chocolate is good for you! Maybe not all good (there are those calories), but studies show that the type of saturated fat in chocolate (stearic acid) does not raise cholesterol levels. Chocolate also contains antioxidants. Therefore, moderate amounts of chocolate are acceptable in most diets, including those for persons with diabetes.

Creamy Lemon Bars

I've seen some terrific low-fat lemon bar recipes. They may be low in fat, but the sugar—wow! There is sugar in the crust, more sugar in the filling, and of course they are topped with even more sugar. My lush lemon bars are a wonderful alternative with less than half of the calories, one third of the fat, and one quarter of the sugar content of the original. Be sure not to overbake or the creamy filling may crack. Enjoy.

CRUST

4	Tbs margarine	½	cup all-purpose flour
2	Tbs brown sugar	½	cup graham cracker crumbs
3	Tbs Splenda Granular		

FILLING

1	cup low fat cottage cheese	½	tsp vanilla
⅓	cup light tub cream cheese	1	Tbs lemon rind
1	cup Splenda Granular	3	Tbs lemon juice
2	Tbs all-purpose flour	1	large egg
½	tsp baking powder	1	large egg white

Preheat oven to 350 degrees. Spray an 8-inch square baking pan with nonstick cooking spray.

In a medium bowl, with an electric mixer, beat the margarine, brown sugar, and Splenda until smooth. Add the flour and graham cracker crumbs and beat on low until blended. Press mixture into the bottom of the prepared pan. Bake for 15 minutes.

While crust is baking prepare topping: Purée cottage cheese until smooth in a food processor. Add the cream cheese and next 6 ingredients. Blend until thick and creamy. Add egg and then egg white, pulsing just briefly to incorporate. Pour filling over hot crust. Return to oven and bake for 18 to 20 minutes, or until cheese mixture appears set. *Twelve servings.*

Per serving:

Calories 140	Fat 6 grams (saturated 2)
Carbohydrate 14 grams (sugar 5)	Fiber 0 grams
Protein 5 grams	Sodium 210 milligrams
Diabetic exchange = 1 bread/starch, 1 medium fat meat	

> Traditional lemon bars use 1½ cups of sugar for the same size recipe, which gives you 24 grams of sugar in one bar!

Apricot Oatmeal Bars

These compact bar cookies are filled with the goodness of oats and the delectable taste of apricot jam. Because these cookies travel well, they would make a nice addition to your next picnic or potluck.

- 1/2 cup all-purpose flour
- 1/2 cup graham cracker crumbs
- 1 cup oats (not instant)
- 1/2 cup Splenda Granular
- 1/3 cup margarine
- 3/4 cup low sugar apricot preserves
- 1 Tbs brown sugar

Preheat oven to 350 degrees. Spray an 8-inch square baking pan with nonstick baking spray.

Place flour and next 4 ingredients in a food processor. Pulse several times until the mixture resembles coarse crumbs. Press two thirds, or about two cups, of the mixture into the prepared baking pan. Bake for 15 minutes. Remove from oven and spread preserves over hot crust. Add the tablespoon of brown sugar to remaining oat mixture, and spread oat layer over jam. Press down lightly on oats layer. Bake for 20 to 25 minutes, or until lightly browned. Cool in pan on wire rack. *Fifteen servings.*

Per serving:

Calories 115
Carbohydrate 17 grams (sugar 7)
Protein 2 grams
Diabetic exchange = 1 carbohydrate, 1 fat

Fat 4 grams (saturated 1)
Fiber 1 gram
Sodium 60 milligrams

You may try any of your favorite low-sugar jams or preserves in these bars.

Frosted Pumpkin Bars

Looking for a new holiday cookie recipe that is healthier than the rest? Here you go—these festive, cake-like, pumpkin bars are sweet, moist, and very delicious. The finishing touch is the rich-tasting cream cheese frosting. All this and half your daily dose of vitamin A—it's enough to make you want to celebrate.

cookie BARS

2	cups all-purpose flour	1½	tsp vanilla
1	tsp baking powder	1	egg
½	tsp baking soda	¼	cup raisins, finely chopped
1½	tsp cinnamon		
½	tsp nutmeg	**FROSTING**	
¼	tsp mace	4	oz. light tub cream cheese
6	Tbs margarine, softened		
3	Tbs baby food prunes	6	oz. non-fat cream cheese
1	15-oz can pumpkin purée		
⅔	cup Splenda Granular	¼	cup Splenda Granular
2	Tbs molasses	2	Tbs orange juice

Preheat oven to 350 degrees. Spray a 9 × 13-inch pan with nonstick baking spray.

Mix together flour, baking powder, baking soda, and spices.

In a large bowl, with an electric mixer, cream the margarine and prunes together. Add pumpkin purée, Splenda, molasses, vanilla, and egg. Beat well. Stir in flour mixture. Stir in raisins. Spoon into prepared pan and smooth. Bake for 20 minutes, or until cake springs back when lightly touched in the center. Cool on rack. In a small bowl, with an electric mixer, beat all frosting ingredients until smooth and fluffy. Spread frosting onto cool bars. Refrigerate. *Twenty-four servings.*

Per serving:

Calories 75
Carbohydrate 8 grams (sugar 3)
Protein 3 grams
Diabetic exchange = ½ carbohydrate, 1 fat

Fat 3.5 grams (saturated 1)
Fiber 0.5 grams
Sodium 120 milligrams

Finely chopping the raisins disperses them better, so you don't need as many.

Raspberry Shortbread Triangles

These cookies remind me of an afternoon tea. They are quite attractive and rather tasty. Because the shortbread really stands out, I use butter in the crust for optimal flavor.

CRUST
- 1 cup all-purpose flour
- 6 Tbs Splenda Granular
- 1/2 tsp lemon rind
- 1/4 cup butter
- 1 Tbs light cream cheese

TOPPING
- 1/2 cup low-sugar preserves
- 1/2 cup fresh or frozen (partially thawed) raspberries
- 1/4 cup Splenda Granular
- 1 large egg white
- 1 tsp butter
- 1/8 tsp almond extract
- 1/3 cup sliced almonds

Preheat oven to 350 degrees. Spray an 8-inch square pan with nonstick baking spray.

In a medium bowl, mix together flour, Splenda, and lemon rind. Cut in butter. Mix in cream cheese until you have fine crumbs. Press onto the bottom of the prepared pan. Bake for 15 minutes.

While crust is baking prepare topping. In a medium bowl, with an electric mixer, beat preserves and next 5 ingredients. Pour over hot, baked crust. Return to oven for 15 minutes longer. Sprinkle almonds evenly over top. Bake 10 minutes longer. Cool on rack 15 minutes. Divide into 9 squares by cutting 3 × 3, then cut each square in half to form 18 triangles. *Nine servings.*

Per serving:

Calories 150
Carbohydrate 19 grams (sugar 7)
Protein 3
Diabetic exchange = 1 carbohydrate, 1 1/2 fat

Fat 7 grams (saturated 4)
Fiber 1 gram
Sodium 65 milligrams

Pies, Crisps, and Cobblers

*M*mm—*nothing makes a home smell better than a pie in the oven. Who can resist the great aroma of a fresh-baked apple pie? Or pumpkin or peach, for that matter. In fact, when you think of good old-fashioned baking, pies often take center stage. Sadly, they are also in the spotlight when naming desserts that are high in sugar, fat, and calories. One culprit here is the crust. A traditional two-crust pie can have 300 calories and over 20 grams of fat in the crust alone. Of course, when you start adding sugar- and fat-laden fillings—watch out! In this chapter, you will learn the trick to making delicious pies that have only a fraction of the fat, calories, and of course, sugar. My stepdaughter, Colleen, had the good fortune to be on spring break the week we tested pies. She reminded me how a great pie can welcome someone into your home. With so many types to choose from, there is always the perfect pie to do the job. From your classic fruit pies and luscious cream pies to rich-tasting no-bake versions, you'll find them all here, along with a warm apple crisp and my favorite, a blackberry cobbler. If you think about it, you can almost smell them baking.*

Single-Crust Pie Pastry
Graham Cracker Pie Crust
Double Chocolate Crumb Crust
Vanilla Wafer Crust
Apple Pie in a Bag
Pumpkin Pie
Fresh Peach Custard Pie
Coconut Cream Pie
Triple Vanilla Cream Pie
Chocolate Mint Cream Pie
Lemon Chiffon Pie
Peanut Butter Pie
Ten-Minute No-Bake Strawberry Cheese Pie
Apple Crisp
Blackberry Cobbler

Single-Crust Pie Pastry

In order to have a great reduced-fat pie, you have to start with a great pie crust. This tasty version has half the fat of some homemade crusts and only one quarter the saturated fat. After many attempts, I found that solid fats work the best to produce a tender crust. The small amount of sugar and the protein in the milk work with the starch to reduce gluten formation and produce a more tender crust. If you are short on time, or simply prefer to use a frozen crust, check the label to find one that has a similar amount of calories, fat, and carbohydrate per serving.

1	cup all-purpose flour
1	Tbs cornstarch
2	tsp sugar
1/4	tsp salt (scant)
2	Tbs shortening
2	Tbs margarine
	(or butter, which adds 1 gram of saturated fat)
2	Tbs ice water
2	Tbs cold 1% milk

Stir together the flour, cornstarch, sugar, and salt in a medium mixing bowl. Cut in the margarine and the shortening, using either a pastry blender or fingers, until all the margarine and shortening is evenly distributed in small crumbs. Mix the milk and the water together and pour onto the flour mixture. Toss the pastry with a fork until it just starts to come together. Using your hands, form the pastry into a ball by gathering up all the flour mixture. (You may add a few more drops of milk or water, if necessary, to pull all the flour together.) Pat the ball into a flat disk and place between two sheets of wax paper. Refrigerate for 30 minutes or longer. Roll dough from center to edge to form an 11-inch circle. Remove paper and gently ease the pastry into a 9-inch pie pan. Press down on pastry to smooth. Patch as needed; turn excess down on edges under and crimp or flute, as desired. *Eight servings.*

To partially bake empty shell: Preheat oven to 425 degrees. Line entire shell, including edges, with aluminum foil, shiny side down, and fill foil with pie weights, rice, or dried beans. Place in bottom third of oven and bake for 10 minutes. Remove the foil and weights, prick the crust with a fork, and return to oven. Bake 10 minutes longer. If air pockets form, open oven and press down on crust with a spoon to flatten. Fill and bake according to recipe directions.

To fully bake empty shell: Preheat oven to 425 degrees. Line bottom and sides of shell with aluminum foil, shiny side down, and fill foil with pie weights, rice, or dried beans. Place in bottom third of oven and bake for 10 minutes. Remove the foil and weights, prick the crust with a fork, return to oven and bake for 12 to 15 minutes more until or until lightly browned. If air pockets form, open oven and press down on crust with a spoon to flatten.

Per serving:

Calories 110
Carbohydrate 13 (sugar 1)
Protein 2 grams
Diabetic exchange = 1 carbohydrate, 1 fat

Fat 6 grams (saturated 1.5)
Fiber 0 grams
Sodium 70 milligrams

The single gram of sugar in this pie pastry helps to keep the crust tender.

Graham Cracker Pie Crust

Versatile and easy—and everyone loves a graham cracker crust. I've lowered the fat by cutting back on the butter and using some egg white to help bind the crust. When purchasing a pre-made graham cracker crust, be sure to look for the low-fat version.

1	cup graham cracker crumbs (about 16 squares)
2	Tbs Splenda Granular
1	Tbs margarine or butter, melted
1	Tbs canola oil
2	Tbs egg white

Preheat oven to 350 degrees. Lightly coat a 9-inch pie pan with non-stick cooking spray.

Combine crumbs in a small bowl or food processor (pulse to make crumbs from crackers). Add Splenda, margarine, and oil, and stir or pulse. Add egg white and stir well, or pulse again. Pour crumb mixture into pie plate. With your fingers, the back of a spoon, or with a sheet of plastic wrap, press down on the crumbs until they coat the bottom and sides of the pie plate. Bake 8 to 10 minutes. Remove and cool. *Eight servings.*

Per serving:

Calories 90
Carbohydrate 12 grams (sugar 7)
Protein 1 gram
Diabetic exchange = 1 carbohydrate, 1 fat

Fat 4.5 grams (saturated 0.5)
Fiber 0 grams
Sodium 105 milligrams

A standard graham cracker crumb crust recipe contains twice the calories, fat, and carbohydrate. And that's before you even start to fill it up!

Double Chocolate Crumb Crust

*T*his is a really good crust. A definite hit with all chocoholics. On my first attempt, I simply used chocolate graham crackers, instead of cookie crumbs, to lower the calories and the sugar content, but I was dismayed at the loss of the deep chocolate flavor. The solution—a bit of cocoa powder to give back the rich chocolate taste, and Splenda to sweeten it up. Chocolate grahams never had it so good.

I   **cup chocolate graham cracker crumbs (about 14 squares)**
I   **Tbs Dutch-process cocoa powder (like Hershey's European)**
¼   **cup Splenda Granular**
I   **Tbs margarine or butter, melted**
I   **Tbs canola oil**
I   **large egg white (about 3 Tbs)**

Preheat oven to 350 degrees. Lightly coat a 9-inch pie pan with non-stick cooking spray.

Combine crumbs in a small bowl or food processor (pulse to make crumbs from crackers). Add cocoa powder, Splenda, margarine, and oil, and stir or pulse. Add egg white and stir well, or pulse again. Pour crumb mixture into pie plate. With your fingers, the back of a spoon, or with a sheet of plastic wrap, press down on the crumbs until they coat the bottom and sides of the pie plate. Bake 8 to 10 minutes. *Eight servings.*

Per serving:

Calories 90
Carbohydrate 12 (sugar 7)
Protein 2 grams
Diabetic exchange = 1 carbohydrate, 1 fat

Fat 4.5 grams (saturated 0.5)
Fiber 0 grams
Sodium 95 milligrams

If you are really watching your carbohydrates, be sure to look closely before substituting a pre-made chocolate crumb crust. They are usually quite a bit higher in sugar and carbohydrates than the graham cracker versions.

Vanilla Wafer Crust

There are actually fewer carbohydrate grams in this simple crust than an ordinary pastry crust. I use this for the Coconut and Triple Vanilla Cream Pies, and it's wonderful. It would also be delicious filled with your favorite chocolate filling.

1	**generous cup crushed vanilla wafers (about 28 wafers)**
1	**Tbs Splenda Granular**
2	**tsp margarine or butter, melted**
1	**Tbs egg white**

Preheat oven to 350 degrees. Lightly coat a 9-inch pie pan with non-stick cooking spray.

Combine crumbs in a small bowl or food processor (pulse to make crumbs from wafers). Add Splenda and margarine, and stir or pulse. Add egg white and stir well, or pulse again. Pour crumb mixture into pie plate. With your fingers, the back of a spoon, or with a sheet of plastic wrap, press down on the crumbs until they coat the bottom and sides of the pie plate. Bake 8 to 10 minutes. *Eight servings.*

Per serving:

Calories 85
Carbohydrate 10 grams (sugar 4)
Protein 1 gram
Diabetic exchange = ½ carbohydrate, 1 fat

Fat 4.5 grams (saturated 1)
Fiber 0 grams
Sodium 60 milligrams

Tip: Place a sheet of plastic wrap down on the crumbs before pressing on them. The crumbs don't stick to the wrap, so it's easy to get them to stick to the pan.

Apple Pie in a Bag

When I was growing up, we used to go to "apple country" every fall. The area produced a cookbook, and one of the most treasured recipes in it was apple pie in a paper bag. It consisted of a one-crust apple pie with a crumb topping that you actually cooked inside a paper grocery bag. The bag helps to re-circulate the steam and imparts a wonderful texture to the apples. Over the years, I've made and eaten the pie many times with no ill effects that I know of. I mention this because the USDA now states that this cooking method may not be safe due to the chemicals and dyes in the paper. My solution—use a cooking bag like the ones used to roast meat. Although I must admit I miss the anticipation of ripping open that paper bag and finding a glorious cooked apple pie inside.

1	Single Crust Pie Pastry, page 66, or prepared crust	**TOPPING**	
6	medium baking apples (about 2½ pounds)	½	cup Splenda Granular
		6	Tbs all-purpose flour
1	Tbs lemon juice	½	tsp cinnamon
6	Tbs Splenda Granular	3	Tbs margarine
1	Tbs all-purpose flour		
½	tsp cinnamon	1	brown-and-serve cooking bag
		1	Tbs all-purpose flour

Preheat oven to 400 degrees. Prepare or set aside one 9-inch unbaked pie pastry shell.

Pare, core, and quarter apples. Halve each quarter crosswise to make chunks. Place in a large bowl and sprinkle with lemon juice. Add 6 tablespoons Splenda, flour, and cinnamon and toss to coat well. Spoon coated apples into shell. Prepare topping: Combine ½ cup Splenda, flour, and cinnamon in a small bowl. Cut in margarine until mixture resembles coarse crumbs.

Sprinkle over the apples, covering entire top of pie. Place 1 tablespoon flour into brown-and-serve bag, and shake. Slide pie into the cooking bag and seal. Place on cookie sheet and place in oven. Bake for 50 minutes or until apples are bubbly and top is browned. Carefully open bag and remove pie. *Eight servings.*

Per serving

Calories 210
Carbohydrate 30 grams (sugar 13)
Protein 2 grams
Diabetic exchange = 1 fruit, 1 carbohydrate, 2 fat

Fat 9 grams (saturated 2.5)
Fiber 2 grams
Sodium 140 milligrams

Pumpkin Pie

It just wouldn't be Thanksgiving without pumpkin pie. This lightened-up version is the perfect ending to a heavy holiday meal. If you prefer your pie to have a lighter, rather than custard-like texture, simply beat the egg whites and fold them in last. The Pumpkin Custard Cups on page 116 features a variation of this same delicious filling prepared in individual soufflé or custard cups to make a delicious creamy custard that eliminates the crust and its calories altogether. (or you can use those "extra savings" on a little more whipped cream topping!)

1	Single Crust Pie Pastry, page 66, or prepared crust	1	large egg white beaten with 2 tsp water

FILLING

1	large egg	1½ tsp	cinnamon
2	egg whites	½ tsp	ginger
1	15-oz can pumpkin purée (not pie filling)	¼ tsp	allspice (optional)
		¼ tsp	ground cloves
¾	cup Splenda Granular	1 tsp	vanilla
1	Tbs molasses	1	12-oz can evaporated skim milk
2	tsp cornstarch		

Preheat oven to 425 degrees. Prepare a partially baked crust according to directions. Remove from oven and immediately brush bottom and sides of the crust with beaten egg white and water mixture. Set aside.

In a large bowl, whisk 1 large egg and egg whites. Add pumpkin, Splenda, molasses, cornstarch, spices, and vanilla. Mix well. Stir in milk. Pour the filling into pre-baked crust. Bake at 425 degrees for 10 minutes, then reduce the heat to 350 degrees and bake 30 to 35 minutes longer, or until a knife inserted near the center comes out clean. Cool pie on wire rack. *Eight servings.*

Per serving:

Calories 200
Carbohydrate 26 (sugar 9)
Protein 8 grams
Diabetic exchange = 1 carbohydrate, 1 fat, ½ low-fat milk, ½ vegetable

Fat 7 grams (saturated 1.5)
Fiber 3 grams
Sodium 160 milligrams

A common problem with pumpkin pies is a soggy crust. A low-fat pie shell only exacerbates the problem. The solution—partially baking and then sealing the crust to keep it crisp.

Fresh Peach Custard Pie

This pie is a sweet burst of summer. Fresh peaches are set into an open crust and covered with a creamy custard. There is just enough custard to hold the peaches together, letting the fresh peach taste shine through.

I	Single Crust Pie Pastry, page 66, or prepared pie crust	1/4	cup non-fat half and half
I	egg white beaten with 2 tsp water	1/2	cup Splenda Granular
I	large egg	2	pounds fresh peaches, peeled and sliced (8 medium peaches)
I	Tbs melted butter or margarine		
I	Tbs all-purpose flour	2	Tbs Splenda Granular
I	Tbs cornstarch	I	Tbs all-purpose flour
1/4	tsp almond extract	I	tsp sugar (optional)

Preheat oven to 425 degrees. Prepare a partially baked pie crust according to directions. Remove from oven and immediately brush bottom and sides of the crust with beaten egg white and water. Set aside.

In a small mixing bowl, whisk together the large egg and next 6 ingredients to make the custard. Set aside. Place the peach slices in a large bowl, and toss with 2 tablespoons Splenda and 1 tablespoon flour. Place peaches into crust. You may arrange them by making circles, starting from the outside of the crust and working your way in, or you can just spoon them in randomly. Pour the custard mixture over the peaches. Place in the oven. Bake at 425 degrees for 10 minutes. Turn oven down to 350 degrees and continue to bake 40 minutes longer, or until the custard appears firmly set when the pan is shaken. Sprinkle 1 teaspoon of sugar for "sparkle" if desired. Let cool on a rack. *Eight servings.*

Per serving:

Calories 190
Carbohydrate 25 grams (sugar 8)
Protein 3 grams
Diabetic exchange = I carbohydrate, 1/2 fruit, 2 fat

Fat 9 grams (saturated 2.5)
Fiber 2 grams
Sodium 135 milligrams

Compare this recipe to a piece of classic Peach Custard Pie which has: 398 calories, 21 grams of fat (13 saturated), 49 carbohydrate, and 26 grams of sugar!

Coconut Cream Pie

I *love this dessert! I rarely eat more than a bite or two of cream pie because I know how very rich they can be. A slice of traditional coconut cream pie can clock in at close to 500 calories. It took more than a trick or two to keep the luscious richness of the original, while using far less sugar and fat. I knew I had accomplished my goal when my neighbor, who has experience as a professional recipe developer, couldn't believe that this pie was not only low in fat but had only two tablespoons of sugar in the entire recipe.*

1 Vanilla Wafer Crust recipe, page 70

FILLING
3/4	cup Splenda Granular
1/4	cup cornstarch
1 1/2	cups 1% milk
1	cup non-fat half-and-half
1	large egg + 1 large egg yolk, lightly beaten
2	tsp coconut extract
1/2	tsp vanilla
2	Tbs coconut

TOPPING
1	Tbs cornstarch
2	Tbs sugar
1/3	up water
6	large, pasteurized egg whites (4 if using regular eggs*)
1/4	tsp cream of tartar
1/2	cup Splenda Granular
3	Tbs coconut

*See Eggs, on page 27 regarding the safety of raw eggs

Preheat oven to 400 degrees.

In a medium saucepan, combine the Splenda and cornstarch. Stir in the milk and half-and-half; whisk until cornstarch completely dissolves. Add beaten eggs and whisk. Bring mixture to a low simmer over medium heat, stirring constantly. As the mixture starts to thicken, remove from heat briefly, and stir thoroughly, including corners, to discourage lumps. Return to heat, simmer, and stir for 1 to 2 minutes. Pudding should be thick and smooth. Stir in extracts and coconut and take off the heat. Pour into the prepared crust and cover with plastic wrap while preparing topping. Place 1 tablespoon cornstarch and sugar into a small saucepan. Add water and stir to form a smooth, thin paste. Place over medium heat and bring to a boil. Stir and boil for 15 seconds. Cover the thick, translucent paste with a lid. In a medium (grease-free) bowl, beat egg whites until foamy. Beat in cream of tartar. Gradually beat in Splenda. Beat until stiff but not dry. Lower speed and beat in all of the cornstarch paste one tablespoon at a time. Increase speed and beat 30 seconds. Remove plastic wrap from pie and cover with meringue. Be sure to cover the pie all the way onto the edges of the crust. Sprinkle the 3 remaining tablespoons of coconut on top. Place in oven and bake 10 minutes, or until coconut toasts and meringue lightly browns. Remove and cool on rack. When completely cool place in the refrigerator. The exterior of the meringue can toughen slightly after a day. *Eight servings.*

Per serving:

Calories 210   Fat 8 grams (saturated 4)
Carbohydrate 28 grams (sugar 12)   Fiber 0 grams
Protein 6 grams   Sodium 150 milligrams
Diabetic exchange = 2 carbohydrate, 1 lean meat, 1 fat

A couple of the tricks used in this recipe:
1) Extracts provide without adding fat, sugar, or calories.
2) In order to make a meringue you need to stabilize the egg whites. The cornstarch/sugar paste makes this possible to do so with a fraction of the sugar normally used in traditional meringue recipes.
Serving tip—cut meringue pie with a serrated knife.

Triple Vanilla Cream Pie

You get not one, not two, but three doses of vanilla in one creamy pie. This easy-to-make cream pie really fills the bill if you enjoy vanilla. After imagining how good vanilla pudding would taste in the Vanilla Wafer Crust, I couldn't resist putting the two together. Add a vanilla-scented cream topping and you've got one delectable pie.

I   **Vanilla Wafer Crust, page 70**
I   **recipe Vanilla Pudding (pie variation) page 114**
1½ **cups light whipped topping, thawed**
½   **tsp vanilla extract**

Prepare crust according to recipe and set aside. Prepare pudding using the pie variation. Pour hot filling into pie crust. Cover surface with plastic wrap. Cool completely on rack, then refrigerate until completely chilled. In a medium bowl combine whipped topping and vanilla extract. Spread over pie. Refrigerate. *Eight servings.*

Per Serving:

Calories 180
Carbohydrate 22 grams (sugar 8)
Protein 4 grams
Diabetic exchange = 1½ carbohydrate, 1 fat, ½ lean meat

Fat 8 grams (saturated 3)
Fiber 0 grams
Sodium 90 milligrams

Chocolate Mint Cream Pie

*O*ne day, while running into the grocery store for a few more testing ingredients, I happened to notice the local Girl Scout troop selling cookies. I wondered if there was anybody who didn't love those Thin Mint cookies. Just then, inspiration struck—the result was Chocolate Mint Cream Pie. This pie has the same winning combination of chocolate and mint. With a dark chocolate crust, creamy chocolate filling, and a mint cream to top it off, who can resist?

1 Double Chocolate Crumb Crust recipe, baked, page 69

FILLING
- ¾ cup Splenda Granular
- 3 Tbs cornstarch
- 2 Tbs Dutch-process cocoa powder
- ½ cup non-fat half-and-half
- 1½ cups 1% milk
- 1 large egg, beaten
- ⅓ cup semi-sweet chocolate chips
- 1 tsp vanilla

TOPPING
- 1½ cup light whipped topping, thawed
- 2 Tbs Splenda Granular
- ¼ tsp mint extract (scant)

In a medium saucepan, combine the Splenda, cornstarch, and cocoa powder. Stir in the milk and half-and-half; whisk until cornstarch completely dissolves. Add the beaten egg and whisk. Bring mixture to a low simmer over medium heat, stirring constantly. As the mixture starts to thicken, remove from heat briefly and stir thoroughly, including corners of the pot to discourage lumps. Add chocolate, return to heat, simmer and stir for 1 to 2 minutes. Pudding should be thick and smooth. Add vanilla, stir, and remove from heat.

Pour hot filling into piecrust. Cover surface with plastic wrap. Cool completely on rack, then refrigerate until completely chilled. In a medium bowl, fold Splenda and mint extract into whipped topping. Spread over pie. Refrigerate.

Flavor variation: Chocolate Peppermint Pie—substitute peppermint extract for mint. *Eight servings.*

Per serving:

Calories 200
Carbohydrate 27 grams (sugar 13)
Protein 5 grams
Diabetic exchange = 2 carbohydrate, 1 lean meat, 1 fat

Fat 8 grams (saturated 4)
Fiber 1 gram
Sodium 150 milligrams

> Dutch-process cocoa powder lends a smoother, richer flavor to recipes than regular cocoa powder does. This is especially important in recipes when there is less sugar and fat to counteract cocoa's bitter side.

Lemon Chiffon Pie

L uscious, and yet so light. This creamy no-bake pie is a nice change from tradi-tional lemon meringue. You actually do make meringue, but rather than plac-ing it on top of the filling, you fold it in. I have chosen to place this pie in a graham cracker crust, but you are welcome to use a pre-baked pastry crust if you prefer.

1 **Graham Cracker Crust recipe, baked, page 68**	¾ **cup Splenda Granular**
	½ **cup lemon juice**
⅓ **cup water**	2 **tsp grated lemon rind**
1 **envelope (2½ tsp) unflavored gelatin**	4 **large pasteurized egg whites (or 2 regular egg whites*)**
1 **large egg + 2 large egg yolks, beaten (reserve whites to use below)**	¼ **tsp cream of tartar**
	3 **Tbs Splenda Granular**
	1 **cup light whipped topping, thawed**

*See Eggs, on page 27 regarding the safety of raw eggs

Place water in a small heavy saucepan and sprinkle gelatin on top. Let set for 3 minutes to soften gelatin. Whisk in beaten eggs, Splenda, lemon juice, and lemon rind. Stirring constantly with a wooden spoon or heat-proof rubber spatula, heat over medium heat until the mixture thickens enough to coat spoon or spatula. Pour the mixture into a large bowl and refrigerate for 45 minutes to 1 hour until mixture mounds when dropped from a spoon, but is not set. In a large bowl, beat egg whites and cream of tartar until foamy. Continue to beat; gradually add Splenda and beat until stiff but not dry. Using a large rubber spatula or spoon, gently fold egg whites into cooled lemon mixture. Fold in whipped topping. Spoon filling into crust and refrigerate for at least 3 hours. *Eight servings.*

Per serving:

Calories 140	Fat 6 grams (saturated 2)
Carbohydrate 18 grams (sugar 9)	Fiber 0 grams
Protein 6 grams	Sodium 145 milligrams
Diabetic exchange = 1 carbohydrate, 1 medium fat meat	

> A traditional lemon chiffon recipe has twice the fat, but that is nothing compared to the sugar. Are you ready for this?—59 grams of carbohydrate, 53 of them from sugar!

Peanut Butter Pie

Although a child could make this easy no-bake pie, it's definitely not just for kids. A Double Chocolate Crumb Crust is filled with a subtle, rich and creamy peanut butter filling and topped with drizzled chocolate. This pie looks and tastes as decadent as it sounds.

1	**Double Chocolate Crumb Crust recipe, baked, page 69**
1/2	**cup low-fat peanut butter**
4	**ounces light tub cream cheese**
4	**ounces fat-free cream cheese**
1/2	**cup Splenda Granular**
1/4	**cup 1% milk**
1/2	**tsp vanilla**
1 1/2	**cups light whipped topping, thawed**
1	**Tbs Chocolate Fudge Sauce, page 132, or**
	2 tsp Hershey's light chocolate syrup

In a large mixing bowl, using an electric mixer, cream the peanut butter and the cream cheeses. Add the Splenda, milk, and vanilla. Beat until smooth. Fold in whipped topping and spoon into crust. Warm fudge sauce and drizzle back and forth across the top of the pie in a decorative fashion. Chocolate syrup need not be warmed. Refrigerate. *Ten servings.*

Per serving:

Calories 205
Carbohydrate 20 (sugar 10)
Protein 7 grams
Diabetic exchange = 1 carbohydrate, 1 medium fat meat, 1 fat

Fat 11 grams (saturated 4)
Fiber 1

Studies have shown that the monounsaturated fats found in peanut butter are good for your health. For die-hard peanut lovers you can add 2 tablespoons more reduced-fat peanut butter. This increases calories by 20, and fat, carbohydrate, and protein by 1 gram each.

Ten-Minute No-Bake Strawberry Cheese Pie

*T*his is simple to make and pretty as a picture to serve. If you want to make it a day ahead, cover the cheese-filled pie and place it in the refrigerator. Within one to two hours of serving time, cover with the fresh berries and glaze.

- **1   low-fat graham cracker crumb crust (store bought)**
- **¹/₂ cup low-fat cottage cheese**
- **4   ounces light cream cheese**
- **¹/₄ cup Splenda Granular**
- **2   Tbs low-sugar strawberry jam, melted**
- **¹/₂ cup light sour cream**
- **1¹/₂ cups strawberry slices, (8 ounces fresh berries)**
- **2   Tbs low-sugar strawberry jam**

Place the cottage cheese in a food processor or blender and purée until entirely smooth.

Pour into a medium bowl and beat in cream cheese, Splenda, and jam with an electric mixer. Stir in sour cream and spoon mixture into crust. Arrange strawberry slices on top of pie in decorative manner to cover top of pie. Melt 2 tablespoons of jam (microwave 20 to 30 seconds on high) and strain by pouring it through a mesh strainer. Brush strained jam over berries. Refrigerate for 1 to 2 hours before serving. *Eight servings.*

Per serving:

Calories 180   Fat 7 grams (saturated 3)
Carbohydrate 22 grams (sugar 12)   Fiber 2 grams
Protein 7 grams   Sodium 260 milligrams
Diabetic exchange = ¹/₂ carbohydrate, ¹/₂ fruit, ¹/₂ low-fat milk, 1 fat

This is a great grab-and-go pie. Remember to keep it cool during your travels.

Apple Crisp

In the autumn, when apples are plentiful and the weather turns cooler, my thoughts turn to apple crisp. With hot tender apples and crispy oat topping, apple crisp is one of life's great comfort foods. Many crisp recipes are low in fat but loaded with sugar, but this one is simply full of apples.

FILLING

2   pounds firm baking apples
     (about 5 medium peeled), cored and cut into ¼ inch slices
2   Tbs orange juice
¼   cup Splenda Granular
1   Tbs all-purpose flour
½   tsp cinnamon

TOPPING

½   cup all-purpose flour
6   Tbs old-fashioned rolled oats
½   cup Splenda Granular
1   tsp cinnamon
4   Tbs light butter

Preheat oven to 350 degrees. Lightly coat an 8 × 8 inch glass baking dish with nonstick cooking spray.

In a large bowl, toss the apples with the orange juice. Mix Splenda, flour, and cinnamon together in a small bowl. Sprinkle over the apples and toss. Place apples in the prepared pan. In a medium bowl, mix together the flour, oats, Splenda, and cinnamon. Cut in butter with a pastry blender, fork, or fingers until mixture resembles fine crumbs. Sprinkle topping over apples. Bake for 40 to 45 minutes, or until apples are tender and crisp is bubbling. Delicious when served warm. *Six servings.*

Per serving:

Calories 175
Carbohydrate 33 grams (sugar 14)
Protein 2 grams
Diabetic exchange = 1 carbohydrate, 1 fruit, 1 fat

Fat 4.5 grams (saturated 2)
Fiber 4 grams
Sodium 20 milligrams

Blackberry Cobbler

There are many versions of cobblers. At one time, it was common to find cobblers made with pie dough, but a sweet, richer type of dough is now the norm. In some recipes, you'll find the dough covers only part of the fruit, and some, like this one, it covers all of it. But any way you make it, cobblers are a fantastic way to eat your fruit.

FILLING		TOPPING	
3	cups blackberries (if frozen, defrost only slightly)	¼	cup 1% milk
		2	tsp lemon juice
¼	cup Splenda Granular	1½	Tbs butter or margarine (melted)
1	Tbs cornstarch	1	cup + 2 Tbs all-purpose flour
1	tsp lemon juice	2	Tbs Splenda Granular
		¾	tsp baking powder
		¼	tsp baking soda
		1	egg white beaten with 2 tsp water
		2	tsp sugar (optional)

Preheat oven to 375 degrees. Lightly coat an 8 × 8-inch glass baking dish or a 9-inch glass pie plate with nonstick cooking spray.

In a large bowl toss the berries lightly with the Splenda, cornstarch, and 1 teaspoon lemon juice. Place in baking dish. In a small bowl, combine the milk, 2 teaspoons lemon juice and the butter. Set aside.

Whisk together the flour, 2 tablespoons Splenda, baking powder, and baking soda in a bowl. Add the milk mixture and mix with a spoon just until the dough comes together.

Gently knead the dough 3 to 4 times until if is soft and uniform. Dust the top and bottom of the dough with a touch of flour and place on a hard surface. Roll or pat the dough gently until it is the size of the top of the baking dish. Brush egg-white mixture over the dough and sprinkle with sugar if desired. Using a knife, make 3 vents by cutting small slits in dough. Bake for 40 to 50 minutes, or until berries are bubbly and crust is brown. Let cool 15 minutes before serving. *Five servings.*

Per serving:

Calories 170
Carbohydrate 29 grams (sugar 7)
Protein 3 grams
Diabetic exchange = 1 carbohydrate, ½ fruit, 1 fat

Fat 4.5 grams (saturated 1)
Fiber 5 grams
Sodium 190 milligrams

Substitute your favorite fruit for the blackberries, or blend fruits together. Mixed berries, peaches and blueberries, or cherries and apples are just a few winning flavor combinations.

Cakes for Any Occasion

*C*akes and celebrations go hand in hand. Whether it be a birthday, holiday, or just for fun, cakes always say, "Let's have a party!" The truth is, for many of us, on those few occasions, we can afford to have the "real thing." But what about those of us who like to celebrate a little more often or of course people who are trying to watch their weight or blood sugar? How often can we afford to splurge and how little does our piece have to be? The answer is not often enough and way too little. Many cakes are unfortunately too high in fat and sugar to enjoy frequently. Not anymore! By lowering the fat and all but a fraction of the sugar in these cakes, you can now create the feel of a party whenever you want. What's more, the portion sizes are normal—no miniscule servings here. So whether you are having a barbeque, a birthday, a kid's party, or a true celebration dinner, now you can have your cake and eat it too!

Applesauce Snack Cake
Orange Sunshine Cupcakes
Unbelievable Chocolate Cake
Fresh Banana Cake
California Carrot Cake with Cream Cheese Frosting
Citrus Chiffon Cake
Lemon Soufflé Cakes
Yogurt Cake
Chocolate Almond Torte
Lemon Coconut Layer Cake

Applesauce Snack Cake

It's no mistake that this is the first cake recipe. Not only is it quick and easy to make, but my true critics, my kids, loved it! I call it a snack cake because it's the perfect kind of cake for an afternoon treat. The cinnamon and sugar topping means no icing is required. Although my kids loved it as it is, I like it served warm with a dollop of light whipped topping.

1/4	cup canola oil	1	tsp baking powder
3/4	cup Splenda Granular	3/4	tsp baking soda
2	Tbs molasses	2	tsp cinnamon
1	large egg	1/2	tsp allspice
3/4	cup unsweetened applesauce	2	tsp sugar
1	tsp vanilla	1	Tbs Splenda Granular
1 1/2	cups all-purpose flour	1/2	tsp cinnamon

Preheat oven to 350 degrees. Spray an 8 × 8-inch cake pan with nonstick baking spray. In a large mixing bowl, stir together the oil, 3/4 cup Splenda, molasses, egg, applesauce and vanilla. Sift in the flour, baking powder, baking soda, and spices and stir until smooth. Spoon batter into prepared pan. In a small bowl, combine the sugar, 1 tablespoon Splenda, and 1/2 teaspoon cinnamon for the topping. Sprinkle with a spoon evenly over the top of the cake. Bake for 20 minutes or until the center of the cake springs back when lightly touched. *Nine servings.*

Per serving:

Calories 170
Carbohydrate 24 grams
Protein 3 grams
Diabetic exchange = 1 1/2 carbohydrate, 1 fat

Fat 7 grams (saturated 0.5)
Fiber 2 grams (sugar 7)
Sodium 170 milligrams

If you want to lower the carbohydrate to one serving and the calories to 130, you can cut this into 12 portions, but a warning—one bite and you won't want a smaller piece!

Orange Sunshine Cupcakes

I developed these tasty cupcakes with luscious, creamy frosting with kids in mind. By the time I was done, I had a cupcake that adults loved just as much. The trickiest part was coming up with a frosting. Although I have seen many reduced-fat frosting recipes. I have never found an icing that doesn't rely heavily on sugar, usually powdered, for both sweetening and bulk. Then I remembered an icing I hadn't made since I was a teenager. You made a flour paste and beat it into a base of granulated sugar and shortening. This would solve the bulk issue. I then lowered the fat by substituting some light cream cheese for some of the shortening and heightened the flavor with a little orange extract. Voilà–a sweet and creamy frosting with only a touch of added sugar.

CUPCAKES

1	cup cake flour	⅔	cup **Splenda Granular**
1	tsp baking powder	1	large egg
½	tsp baking soda	1	tsp vanilla
2	Tbs margarine	¼	cup 1% milk
2	Tbs canola oil	⅓	cup unsweetened orange juice
Whipped Frosting, page 86			

Preheat oven to 325 degrees. Spray 8 muffin cups with nonstick baking spray. Sift the cake flour with the baking powder and baking soda. Set aside. In a large bowl, cream the margarine and oil with an electric mixer. Add Splenda, egg, and vanilla and beat well. By hand stir in half of flour mixture to the creamed ingredients. Add the milk and mix until smooth. Stir in the remaining flour and finish with the orange juice. Spoon into the prepared pans, filling ⅔ full. Bake for 15 minutes or until cupcakes spring back when lightly touched in the center. Remove from oven and cool. *Eight servings.*

WHIPPED FROSTING

1/2	cup 1% milk	1	cup **Splenda Granular**
2	Tbs all-purpose flour	2	Tbs powdered sugar
2	Tbs vegetable shortening	1/2	tsp orange extract
4	oz light tub cream cheese		

Prepare frosting: Pour milk into a small pot and add flour. Stir until smooth with no lumps. Place over low heat and cook until a smooth, thick paste forms. Set aside to cool slightly. Place shortening and cream cheese in a small mixing bowl. Beat at high speed with an electric mixer until creamy. Beat in Splenda. Add flour paste and continue to beat until smooth and creamy. Add powdered sugar and extract. Frost each cooled cupcake with 1½ tablespoon of frosting. You will use most but not all of the frosting.

Per serving:

Calories 170
Carbohydrate 17 grams (sugar 4)
Protein 2 grams
Diabetic exchange = 1 carbohydrate, 2 fat

Fat 9 grams (saturated 3)
Fiber 0 grams
Sodium 210 milligrams

This recipe can easily be doubled if you need a bigger batch of cupcakes.

Unbelievable Chocolate Cake

*N*o *one could ever guess a chocolate cake so moist and light, tender and delicious, could have so little fat and sugar. As if that weren't enough, it only takes one bowl, a whisk, and ten minutes to whip this cake together. It took me several attempts to get this one right and it was definitely worth it! Keeping in a small amount of brown sugar made all the difference. Believe me, a cake like this with only ¼ cup of sugar is, well, unbelievable.*

¼ **cup canola oil**	1 **tsp baking powder**
1 **large egg**	¼ **cup Dutch-process cocoa**
1 **tsp vanilla**	**powder (like Hershey's**
¼ **cup brown sugar, packed**	**European)**
(be sure it is fresh, with	¼ **cup hot water**
no hard lumps)	2 **tsp powdered sugar**
1 **cup Splenda Granular**	**(optional)**
1 **cup low-fat buttermilk**	
1¼ **cups cake flour**	**Chocolate Cream Frosting,**
1 **tsp baking soda**	**page 135 (optional)**

Preheat oven to 350. Spray an 8 × 8-inch baking pan with nonstick cooking spray. In a large bowl whisk together the oil and the egg for 1 minute until the mixture is thick and frothy. Add the vanilla, brown sugar, and Splenda and beat with the whisk for 2 more minutes until the mixture is thick and smooth and the sugars have been thoroughly beaten into the mixture. Add 1 cup buttermilk and mix. Using a sifter or a metal sieve, sift the flour, baking powder, baking soda, and cocoa powder into the liquid mixture. Whisk vigorously for 1 to 2 minutes until the batter is nice and smooth. Pour the hot water into the batter and whisk one more time until the batter is again nice and smooth. The batter will be thin. Pour the batter into the prepared cake pan and tap the pan on the counter to level the surface and to help remove any air bubbles. Bake for 18 to 20 minutes or just until the center springs back when touched and a cake tester or toothpick comes out clean. Do not overcook. Remove the cake from the oven and cool. Sift optional powder sugar over cake to serve. *Nine servings.*

Per serving:

Calories 160
Carbohydrate 22 grams (sugar 8)
Protein 3 grams
Diabetic exchange = 1½ servings carbohydrate, 1 fat

Fat 7 grams (saturated 1)
Fiber 1 grams
Sodium 200 milligrams

> I love this cake dusted with powdered sugar and served with light topping and sliced strawberries. It's also delicious topped with Chocolate Cream Frosting, page 135.

Fresh Banana Cake

*E*very time I have some overripe bananas, I think of this cake. The recipe is easy and practically foolproof. I have made it many times using sugar and am happy to report it is just as wonderful without it. It's so moist it is hard to believe there is so little fat in it.

3	small bananas, mashed (about 1 cup purée)	½	cup nonfat plain yogurt
2	Tbs canola oil	2	tsp vanilla
⅔	cup Splenda Granular	1½	cups cake flour
1	Tbs molasses	1	tsp baking powder
1	large egg	¾	tsp baking soda
1	large egg white	2	tsp powdered sugar (optional)

Preheat oven to 350 degrees. Spray a 9-inch cake pan with nonstick baking spray. Place banana purée in a large mixing bowl. Whisk in next 7 ingredients (oil through vanilla). Sift cake flour, baking powder, and baking soda into the bowl. Stir to blend in dry ingredients.

Spoon batter into prepared pan. Bake for 30 minutes or until a toothpick inserted into the center of the cake comes out clean. Cool in pan. Sift powdered sugar over cake just prior to serving if desired. *Eight servings.*

Per serving:

Calories 130
Carbohydrate 21 grams (sugar 7)
Protein 3 grams
Diabetic exchange = 1½ carbohydrate, ½ fat

Fat 3.5 (saturated 0)
Fiber 1 gram
Sodium 300 milligrams

This a great old-fashioned homestyle cake. When serving it to guests, I warm it up and then top each piece with a spoonful of light whipped topping and a few slices of fresh banana.

California Carrot Cake with Cream Cheese Frosting

*A*s *a child, I remember my Mom making this popular cake. I'm sure she thought it was nice to have such a delicious treat be good for you, too. What she didn't realize is that her famed carrot cake—made with lots of oil and sugar—was loaded with fat and calories. My version retains the same moist, sweet quality of the original. Prune purée and buttermilk are great substitutes for most of the oil, and Splenda works beautifully as the sweetener. Topped with a delicious cream cheese frosting, this cake—with 2 grams of fiber and almost a day's worth of vitamin A—really is a healthy treat.*

I	cup all-purpose flour	1/4	cup canola oil
I	cup wheat flour	I	large egg
2	tsp baking soda	3	large egg whites
I	tsp baking powder	I	tsp vanilla
2	tsp cinnamon	3/4	cup low-fat buttermilk
1/2	tsp nutmeg	1 1/2	cups Splenda Granular
1/4	tsp cloves	8	ounces crushed pineapple, packed in unsweetened juice
1/3	cup chopped nuts	1 1/2	cups peeled and shredded carrots
1/4	cup prune purée		

Light Cream Cheese Frosting, page 90

Preheat oven to 350 degrees. Coat a 9 × 12-inch cake pan with nonstick cooking spray.

In a medium bowl, combine the flours, baking soda, baking powder, spices, and chopped nuts. Stir to blend. In a large bowl, measure the prune purée, oil, vanilla, and eggs. Whisk together. Add the buttermilk and Splenda. Whisk. Stir in the pineapple (including juice) and carrots. Add the flour mixture. Stir to form batter. Transfer the batter into prepared pan. Bake for 25 to 30 minutes, or until a toothpick inserted in the center of the cake comes out clean. Let the cake cool in the pan. Frost with the light cream cheese frosting. *Fifteen servings.*

LIGHT CREAM CHEESE FROSTING
8   ounces light tub cream cheese
4   ounces non-fat cream cheese
¼   cup Splenda Granular
I   cup light whipped topping

In a small mixing bowl, beat the cream cheeses together with an electric mixer until smooth. Add the Splenda and beat for 1 minute longer. On slow speed, beat in the whipped topping and mix frosting briefly until smooth.

Per serving:

Calories 200   Fat 9 grams (saturated 3)
Carbohydrate 24 grams (sugar 6)   Fiber 2 grams
Protein 7 grams   Sodium 300 milligrams
Diabetic exchange = I carbohydrate, ½ fruit, 2 fat

Most low-fat carrot cakes are still high in sugar due to the icing as well as the cake. Most average 65 to 75 grams of carbohydrate per piece.

Citrus Chiffon Cake

A chiffon cake is a terrific cake made from a cake-like batter and lightened with egg whites. It's technically in a class of cakes called foam cakes. Like its cousin, the angel food cake, the light chiffon cake is moist and often served with fresh fruit or fruit sauces. It slices and freezes well, which adds to its versatility as a great cake for entertaining. Keep one in your freezer and you'll always be ready for unexpected company.

2 1/4 cups cake flour	3/4 cup unsweetened orange juice
1 Tbs baking powder	zest of 1 orange
1/2 tsp salt	zest of 1 lemon
1 1/4 cups Splenda Granular	8 egg whites
3 egg yolks	1/2 tsp cream of tartar
1/3 cup canola oil	

Preheat the oven to 325 degrees. Set aside one 10-inch ungreased tube pan with a removable bottom (an angel food cake pan).

Sift together the cake flour, baking powder, and salt. Stir in the Splenda. Set aside.

In a large bowl, beat the yolks, oil, orange juice, and zest with an electric mixer at high speed until smooth. Incorporate the flour mixture on low speed. In a separate, large, grease-free bowl, whip the egg whites and cream of tartar until soft peaks form. Fold in 1/4 of the egg whites into the batter. Carefully fold in the remaining whites. Spoon the batter into the pan and smooth. Bake for 45 to 50 minutes or until the top springs back when lightly pressed. Let cool upside down at least 1 1/2 hours. *Fourteen servings.*

Per serving:

Calories 140
Carbohydrate 16 grams (sugar 2)
Protein 4 grams
Diabetic exchange = 1 carbohydrate, 1 fat

Fat 6 grams (saturated 5)
Fiber 0 grams
Sodium 140 milligrams

This cake is delicious served with Blueberry Sauce; see page 129.

Lemon Soufflé Cakes

These really should be called "mistake cakes." I was trying to develop a lemon pudding cake and wound up with these incredible delectables. A lemon pudding cake, when baked forms a small layer of lemon pudding under the cake. Realizing that the granulated sugar in the recipe contributed to both the rise of the batter and to the thickening of the pudding, I added a little cornstarch and a touch of baking powder to compensate for the switch to Splenda. What came out of the oven was a cake, but no pudding was to be found. I thought it was a loss until I tasted what I thought would be a disaster. It was very tasty and had a moist but airy texture that reminded me of a fallen soufflé. I tried the recipe again, this time using 6-ounce ramekins to produce individual cakes. They were a hit. These would make a nice dessert for a dinner for four. You can get the ramekins ready ahead of time and pop them in the oven while you eat. Serve them with a touch of light whipped topping and blueberries for a spectacular finish.

4	large egg whites	1/4	cup lemon juice
3	Tbs Splenda Granular	1	Tbs lemon rind
1	Tbs granulated sugar	1/4	cup all-purpose flour
2	large egg yolks	1	tsp cornstarch
1	Tbs butter or margarine	1/4	tsp baking powder
3/4	cup Splenda Granular	2	tsp granulated sugar
3/4	cup low-fat buttermilk		

Preheat oven to 350 degrees. Spray four 6-ounce ramekins or soufflé cups with nonstick cooking spray and place them in a larger baking pan that is at least 2 inches deep; set aside.

In a deep bowl, beat egg whites with an electric mixer on high speed until foamy. Beat in the Splenda and 1 tablespoon of granulated sugar until soft peaks form when beaters are lifted from the whites. In another bowl, combine eggs yolks, butter, and Splenda and beat until thick and creamy. Stir in the next 6 ingredients and beat until smooth. Fold in one quarter of the egg whites; stir to incorporate. Gently fold in remaining egg whites. Divide the batter into the ramekins (3/4 full). Sprinkle 1/2 teaspoon of granulated sugar on top of each cake and place baking dish on middle rack of the oven. Pour boiling water into the dish until the water reaches half-way up the ramekins. Bake for 25 to 30 minutes or until center feels firm to the touch. They are done as soon as the center sets. *Four servings.*

Per Serving:

Calories 160	Fat 5 grams (saturated 2)
Carbohydrate 20 grams (sugar 8)	Fiber 0 grams
Protein 7 grams	Sodium 130 milligrams
Diabetic exchange = 1 1/2 carbohydrate, 1 medium fat meat	

Yogurt Cake

When I first started teaching the principles of healthy cooking, not many chefs agreed that low-fat cooking could be synonymous with great food. A decade later, many highly respected chefs have adopted the idea that healthy cooking techniques can indeed produce good food. One of those chefs is the world-renowned Jaques Pepin, whose own healthy cookbook, Simple and Healthy Cooking, *inspired me to produce this Yogurt Cake. It is a basic moist white cake.*

1	cup + 2 Tbs cake flour	⅔	cup Splenda Granular
1½	tsp baking powder	1	tsp vanilla extract
¼	tsp baking soda	¼	tsp almond extract
3	large egg whites	1	large egg
3	Tbs granulated sugar	½	cup plain non-fat yogurt
3	Tbs canola oil	⅓	cup unsweetened apple-sauce

Preheat oven to 350 degrees. Spray a 8-inch round cake pan with non-stick baking spray.

Sift the flour with the baking powder and soda and set aside. In a medium bowl, beat egg whites until frothy. Gradually add the 3 tablespoons of sugar; continue to beat until soft peaks form when the mixer is lifted from the whites. Set aside. In a large bowl, cream the oil and the Splenda. Add the next 5 ingredients and beat for 1 to 2 minutes. (It may not look totally creamy.) Sift the flour with the baking powder and soda and add to the bowl. Beat until smooth. Gently fold in the beaten egg whites. Spoon the batter into the prepared pan. Bake for 20 minutes or until center of the cake springs back when lightly touched. *Eight servings.*

Per serving:

Calories 150
Carbohydrate 16 grams (sugar 5)
Protein 4 grams
Diabetic exchange = 1 carbohydrate, 1 fat

Fat 6.0 grams (saturated 0.5)
Fiber 0 grams
Sodium 190 milligrams

This would be especially nice topped with a touch of powdered sugar and some fresh fruit.

Chocolate Almond Torte

In Austria and Germany, the word torte *refers to any round cake. Torte also refers to cakes that use ground nuts or bread crumbs in place of some or most of the flour. When made with chocolate, cakes that are sparse on flour and heavy on egg whites are commonly referred to as flourless chocolate cakes. Dense and moist, this is one special cake. Serve it dusted with powdered sugar, or with the Quick Raspberry Sauce recipe on page 131, for an elegant dessert. My personal favorite is to warm the cake, then place each slice on top of a pool of raspberry sauce and top it with light whipped topping. Yum.*

3/4	cup semisweet chocolate morsels	2	Tbs cocoa powder
3	Tbs hot water	1/4	tsp baking powder
1/3	cup prune purée	5	egg whites
1/2	tsp almond extract	1/3	cup Splenda Granular
1/2	cup almonds, toasted	1/2	tsp cream of tartar
1/4	cup all-purpose flour	2	tsp powdered sugar
1/2	cup Splenda Granular		(optional)

Preheat oven to 375 degrees. Spray bottom of an 8-inch round spring-form or cake pan with nonstick baking spray. Toast almonds by placing on a pie plate and baking for 5 minutes.

Melt chocolate in a small pan over hot water or place in a bowl and microwave for 1½ minutes. Stir until all chips are melted. Stir in hot water, prune purée, and almond extract. Using a food processor grind nuts. Add flour, ½ cup Splenda, cocoa powder, and baking powder. Mix flour mixture into the chocolate. In a separate bowl, beat egg whites and cream of tartar until frothy. Gradually add ⅓ cup of Splenda and beat until soft peaks form. Fold ⅓ of egg whites into cool chocolate mixture to lighten mixture. Gently fold in remaining whites. Spoon mixture into prepared pan. Smooth and place in oven. Bake for 20 to 22 minutes until center is just set. Do not over-bake. Cool in pan for 30 minutes. Dust with sugar. *Eight servings.*

Per serving:

Calories 190
Carbohydrate 24 (sugar 10)
Protein 4 grams
Diabetic exchange = 1½ carbohydrate, 2 fat

Fat 9 grams (saturated 2.5)
Fiber 3 grams
Sodium 50 milligrams

Traditional European tortes are ultrarich in eggs, butter, chocolate and nuts. A similar cake would contain 460 calories, 29 grams of fat, and 45 grams of carbohydrate per serving.

Lemon Coconut Layer Cake

*H*ere's a birthday cake for those who love lemon desserts (like me!). A simple white layer cake is split, then filled and frosted with a sumptuous lemon cream frosting. You can prepare the lemon curd far in advance of the cake and frosting, which will make putting this together a snap. I found it held very well in the refrigerator for several days. Enjoy.

3	egg whites	I	cup + 2 Tbs cake flour
2	Tbs granulated sugar	2	tsp baking powder
3	Tbs canola oil	¼	tsp baking soda
I	tsp vanilla	½	cup lemon curd, page 133
½	cup low-fat buttermilk	1¼	cups light whipped topping
⅔	cup Splenda Granular	⅓	cup shredded coconut
I	large egg		

Preheat oven to 350 degrees. Spray an 8-inch cake pan with nonstick baking spray or line pan bottom with wax paper. In a medium bowl, beat 3 egg whites until frothy. Gradually add sugar and continue to beat until soft peaks form when the mixer is lifted from the whites. Set aside.

On medium speed, mix oil, vanilla, buttermilk, Splenda, and egg in a large bowl. Sift together the cake flour, baking powder, and baking soda into the bowl and blend until smooth. Gently fold in the beaten egg whites. Spoon into prepared pan and smooth top. Bake for 20 minutes or until the center springs back when lightly touched. Cool cake in pan on rack for 10 minutes. Loosen cake from pan by inverting briefly. Let cake layer cool completely.

Set cake on plate and slice in half horizontally to make two layers. Mix the lemon curd and the whipped topping together in a bowl. Place ½ cup of frosting on the first layer of the cake. Place second layer on top and frost top and sides with the remaining frosting. Sprinkle coconut over the top of the cake. Refrigerate until served. *Eight servings.*

Per serving:

Calories 175
Carbohydrate 22 (sugar 7)
Protein 4 grams
Diabetic exchange = 1½ carbohydrate, 1½ fat

Fat 8 grams (saturated 1.5)
Fiber 0 grams
Sodium 200 milligrams

Cheesecakes to Die For

There are always fabulous, rich desserts that come and go in popularity. One dessert, however, that continues to be a favorite year in and year out is cheesecake. Whether it's served at your local diner or the most elegant restaurant in town, it's rich and creamy, delicious and decadent. When people go out, they like to have fun; when they splurge on a dessert—you've got it— it's cheesecake. Of course, the idea that they are splurging probably comes from the fact that just one piece of that classic New York Cheesecake contains over 600 calories, with most of the calories coming from fat (and plenty of that is saturated). The great thing about making your own cheesecakes, besides how incredible they taste, is that are simple to make. By making them yourself, you can successfully eliminate as much they as 75 percent of the fat and almost all of the sugar (Splenda is incredible for cheesecakes). So go ahead, impress your family and friends with mouthwatering cheesecakes like Luscious Lemon, Mocha Chip, and Key Lime that average a mere 200 calories a slice, and get ready to splurge!

Cheesecake Crumb Crust
Heavenly Cheesecake
Luscious Lemon Cheesecake
Strawberry Swirl Cheesecake
Chocolate Cheesecake
Mocha Chip Cheesecake
Pumpkin Streusel Cheesecake

No-Bake Cheesecakes:
Cheesecake Parfait
Key Lime Cheesecake
Chocolate Peppermint Cheesecake

Cheesecakes 101

A cheesecake isn't really a cake at all; it's a custard. Like custard, baked cheese-cakes rely on eggs, which set into a solid gel when cooked. This creates a "cake" firm enough to slice. Because this cake is made from cream cheese and other dairy products, rather than flour, it has a silky, smooth texture.

Comparing Cheesecakes*

Cheesecake	Calories	Fat grams	Saturated fat grams	Carbohydrate grams	Sugar grams	Protein grams
Regular Cheesecake	560	40	23	40	34	9
Reduced-Fat Cheesecake	420	23	14	44	36	10
Heavenly Cheesecake (page 102)	180	8	5	15	7	11

*¹/₁₂ of a 9-inch cheesecake

The number-one culprit for fat and calories in cheesecake is cream cheese. It contains nearly 800 calories and 80 grams of fat (50 of it satu-rated) per 8-ounce package. A single cheesecake can call for three or more packages. Additional high fat, saturated fat, and calorie contributors are full-fat sour cream and eggs. Sugar is fat-free but contains 775 calories and 200 grams of carbohydrate per cup.

- A cheesecake made entirely from *reduced* fat products has a third less fat and fewer calories—and can taste great. Unfortunately, this version still contains over 400 calories and 23 grams of fat per serving. It also contains a whopping 36 grams—or the equivalent of 8 teaspoons—of sugar per slice!

- A cheesecake made entirely from *non-fat* products tastes non-fat and does not have the mouthfeel of regular cheesecake.

- A blend of creamed low-fat cottage cheese, low-fat cream cheese, and non-fat cream cheese in cheesecakes (to replace 24 ounces of full-fat cream cheese), gives wonderful texture and flavor with two-thirds fewer calories and 20 percent of the fat! Sugar is no longer an issue if you use Splenda—and it works great.

- Everyone that has made cheesecakes knows about cracks. They are the annoying earthquake lines (or so it seems) that can form on the top of the cake. The major causes of cracks include excessive oven temperatures, overcooking, and overbeating the batter. Cracks may be covered with fruit, fruit toppings, or sweetened sour cream.

Cooking Tips

Cheesecakes are the perfect party dessert. They are easy to make, everybody loves them, and are actually better if they are made a day or two in advance. The following tips, including two different ways to cook your cheesecake, will help you produce a perfect cheesecake every time.

Pans
Springform pans are used to bake cheesecakes to allow the entire cake to be easily removed from the pan for serving. You may substitute a regular cake pan to bake the cake with no ill effects.

Creaming Cottage Cheese
To cream the cottage cheese, place in a food processor and blender and purée on high speed. It is finished when there are *no* curds left. It will look smooth. The chefs I've taught love this trick and have used this as a replacement for mayonnaise and/or sour cream.

Cream Cheese
Have the cream cheeses at room temperature before beating. Do not add the eggs or any liquid until the cheeses are beaten together and are smooth. If eggs or liquid are added too soon, cream cheese can form into lumps that will not smooth out. The cheesecake will still taste terrific but the lumps may show.

Beating
Do not overbeat the batter. It can contribute to cracking. It is especially important to stop beating after the eggs have been incorporated into the batter.

Cooking in a Water Bath
The water bath cooking method is the best insurance against cracking. It controls excessive heat and produces a cheesecake that is uniformly creamy from edge to center. When baking the cake in a springform pan, you must first seal the pan so that water will not seep into the cake. Set the pan on several sheets of aluminum foil (or one sheet if heavy duty) and fold the foil up the sides of

the pan, securing at the top rim. Place the foil-wrapped unbaked cheesecake in a baking pan that is at least 3 inches wider than the cheesecake pan (a roasting dish works great). Set the roasting or baking pan on the pre-heated oven rack. Carefully pour very hot or boiling water halfway up the outside of the cheesecake pan. Gently slide the oven rack into the oven and bake for as long as directed. Cheesecakes cooked in regular cake pans do not need to be wrapped in foil.

Cooking the "Traditional" Way

The traditional cooking method bakes the cheesecake at a temperature that is low enough to encourage even heating. (300 to 325 degrees). For this method to work without producing cracks, you must be extremely careful not to over-beat the batter or overcook the cheesecake. In addition, you must cool the cake slowly. If you want the edges of your cheesecake to be dryer and denser than the creamy center, this is the method for you. When the cheesecake is ready to be baked, simply place in the center of the oven.

Cooking Time

With either method, you need to know when the cheesecake is done. When finished, the cheesecake should appear firm around the edges, but the very center should still jiggle slightly when the pan is shook. Cheesecakes do not completely set until cooled.

Cooling

The best way to cool cheesecakes is to leave them in the oven for 30 to 60 minutes after baking. Turn off the oven and prop the door open to slowly reduce the oven temperature. This ensures the cheesecake is not "shocked" by the temperature change, which can result in cracking.

Cheesecake Crumb Crust

This crumb crust is very similar to the one I use for pies. Because cheese-cakes do not require a crust on the sides less crumbs are needed. Cheesecake fillings also tend to seep into the crust and help to bind it togeth-er which eliminates the need for some of the fat and the egg white used in gra-ham crusts used for pies. In order to keep the fillings from seeping too much and creating a soggy crust, the crust is baked separately before filling.

- ¾ **cup graham cracker crumbs (about 12 squares)**
- 2 **Tbs Splenda Granular**
- 1 **Tbs margarine or butter, melted**

Preheat oven to 350 degrees. Spray an 8- or 9-inch springform pan, as specified in cheesecake recipe, with nonstick cooking spray.

If starting with whole graham crackers, place them in a blender or food processor and pulse to make fine crumbs. Place the crumbs in a bowl and add Splenda and melted butter or margarine. Stir to mix. Pour the crumb mixture into the bottom of the prepared pan. With your fingers, the back of a spoon, or a sheet of plastic wrap, press down on the crumbs to cover the bottom of the pan. Bake for 5 minutes. Cool. (Be sure the crust is *completely* cool when using for unbaked cheesecakes.)

Variation: Chocolate Crumb Crust. Substitute chocolate graham crack-ers for the regular grahams. Add 1 teaspoon of cocoa powder along with the Splenda and butter or margarine to the crumbs. *Twelve servings.*

Per serving:

Calories 40
Carbohydrate 6 grams (sugar 3)
Protein 0 grams
Diabetic exchange = ½ carbohydrate

Fat 1.5 grams (saturated 0.5)
Fiber 0 grams
Sodium 55 milligrams

The Pumpkin Streusel Cheesecake uses Gingersnap Cookies instead of graham crackers for a unique flavor combination.

Heavenly Cheesecake

This was the cheesecake in my family when I was growing up, made only for special occasions and much savored over. I really wanted my makeover to work on this one—and it did! One bite and I knew. But of course, I needed another opinion. A good friend and her husband just happened to be coming over for dinner a couple of days after I made this (it holds beautifully) so I served it up for dessert. One bite and my friend exclaimed, "This is my cheesecake. I can't believe it!" As a bride, she had received a very special gift— a cheesecake recipe! She was sure this was her recipe. In fact, when after comparing her recipe to my original they were almost identical. The real surprise, however, came when she found out that this lightened version had only a third of the calories, less than half of the carbohydrate and one-fifth of the fat of our original recipes. That's what I call "heavenly." (See page 98 for the nutritional comparison.)

1	8- or 9-inch baked Cheesecake Crumb Crust, page 101	2	Tbs all-purpose flour
1	cup low-fat cottage cheese	2	Tbs cornstarch
8	oz tub-style light cream cheese	1	tsp vanilla extract
8	oz non-fat cream cheese, room temperature	1/2	tsp almond extract
		1	large egg
		3	large egg whites
1 1/4	cups Splenda Granular	1 1/4	cups light sour cream

Preheat oven to 350 degrees. Wrap 8-inch (or 9-inch) springform pan with crust tightly in heavy-duty foil to make waterproof.

Place cottage cheese into a food processor or blender. Purée until completely smooth. Spoon into a large mixing bowl and add nonfat and light cream cheeses. Beat on medium speed, with an electric mixer until creamy. Add the Splenda, flour, cornstarch, and extracts, and beat on low until smooth. Add large egg and then egg whites beating just briefly after each addition to incorporate. Stir in the sour cream with a large spoon. Pour into the prepared crust and smooth top. Place the foil-wrapped pan in a large, deep baking pan and pour boiling water into pan until it reaches halfway up the outside of the cheesecake pan. Bake for 60 minutes or until sides of cake appear firm and center jiggles slightly. (For a 9-inch pan, bake 50 to 55 minutes.) Turn off heat, open oven door, and let cheesecake cool in the oven for 30 minutes. Remove from water bath and finish cooling. Refrigerate at least 6 hours before serving. *Twelve servings.*

Per serving:

Calories 180   Fat 8 grams (saturated 5)
Carbohydrate 15 grams (sugar 7)   Fiber 0 grams
Protein 11 grams   Sodium 350 milligrams
Diabetic exchange = 1 carbohydrate, 1½ lean meat

A wonderful compliment to this cheesecake is the Strawberry Coulis on page 130. If you prefer a sour cream topping, simply spread the cake with a mixture of ½ cup light sour cream and 2 tablespoons Splenda as you turn off the heat. Allow to cool in oven as directed.

Luscious Lemon Cheesecake

The name says it all. This cheesecake is sure to please. I sent my husband to work with this luscious creation and the cake was quickly gobbled up. No one ever suspected it wasn't a "regular" cheesecake. Mission accomplished.

1	9-inch baked Cheesecake Crumb Crust, page 101	2	tsp cornstarch
1	cup low-fat cottage cheese	2	tsp lemon juice
8	oz tub-style light cream cheese	1	Tbs lemon zest
8	oz non-fat cream cheese, room temperature	1	8-oz carton non-fat lemon yogurt (not light)
1	cup Splenda Granular	2	large eggs
2	Tbs all-purpose flour	2	large egg whites

Preheat oven to 350 degrees. Wrap 9-inch springform pan with crust tightly in heavy-duty foil (to make waterproof).

Place cottage cheese into a food processor or blender. Purée until completely smooth. Spoon into a large mixing bowl and add nonfat and light cream cheeses. Beat on medium speed with an electric mixer until creamy. Add the Splenda, flour, and cornstarch, and beat on low until smooth. Blend in the lemon juice, zest, and yogurt. Add whole eggs and then egg whites, beating briefly after each addition to incorporate. Pour into the prepared pan and smooth top. Place the foil-wrapped pan in a large, deep baking pan and pour boiling water into pan until it reaches halfway up the outside of the cheesecake pan. Bake for 60 to 65 minutes or until sides of cake appear firm and center jiggles slightly. Turn off the heat, open oven door and let cheesecake cool down in the oven for 30 minutes. Remove from water bath and finish cooling on rack. Refrigerate at least 6 hours before serving. *Twelve servings.*

Per serving:

Calories 160	Fat 6 grams (saturated 3.5)
Carbohydrate 15 grams (sugar 5)	Fiber 0 grams
Protein 10 grams	Sodium 340 milligrams
Diabetic exchange = 1 carbohydrate 1½ lean meat	

> Serve this cake with fresh strawberries. I like to slice them in half lengthwise and cover the entire top.

Strawberry Swirl Cheesecake

This is one gorgeous cheesecake. It is covered with a marbled strawberry topping that bakes right into the cheesecake. Because you can make it with either fresh or frozen strawberries, it can be enjoyed year-round.

1 9-inch baked Cheesecake Crumb Crust, page 101	8 oz non-fat cream cheese, room temperature
1¼ cups fresh or frozen unsweetened strawberries	1¼ cups Splenda Granular
2 Tbs low-sugar strawberry jam	2 Tbs all-purpose flour
2 Tbs Splenda Granular	2 Tbs cornstarch
2 tsp lemon juice	1 tsp vanilla extract
1 cup low-fat cottage cheese	½ tsp almond extract
8 oz tub-style light cream cheese	1 large egg
	3 large egg whites
	1¼ cups light sour cream

Preheat oven to 350 degrees. Wrap 9-inch springform pan with crust tightly in heavy-duty foil to waterproof.

Combine the strawberries, jam, Splenda, and lemon juice in a medium saucepan. Stir and cook until strawberries are soft and mushy. Use a fork to mash berries completely to form a thick strawberry purée (may use a food processor or blender). Set mixture aside to cool.

Place cottage cheese into a food processor or blender. Purée until completely smooth. Spoon into a large mixing bowl and add nonfat and light cream cheeses. Beat on medium speed with an electric mixer until creamy. Add the Splenda, flour, cornstarch, and extracts. Beat on low until smooth. Add whole egg and then egg whites, beating briefly after each addition to incorporate. Stir in the sour cream with a large spoon. Pour into the prepared pan and smooth top. Carefully place spoonfuls of the strawberry purée on top of the batter. Swirl a thin knife back and forth through the purée and batter to create a marbleized effect. Place foil-wrapped pan in a large, deep baking pan and place on oven rack. Pour boiling water into pan until it reaches halfway up the outside of the cheesecake pan. Bake for 70 to 75 minutes or until sides of cake appear firm and center jiggles slightly. Turn off heat, open oven door, and let cheesecake cool in the oven for 30 minutes. Remove from water bath and finish cooling. Refrigerate at least 6 hours before serving. *Twelve servings.*

Per serving:

Calories 190
Carbohydrate 17 grams (sugar 8)
Protein 11 grams
Diabetic exchange = 1 carbohydrate, 1½ lean meat

Fat 8 grams (saturated 5)
Fiber 1 gram
Sodium 350 milligrams

Chocolate Cheesecake

*C*heesecake *and chocolate—how much better can it get? This creamy cake is for all you chocolate lovers. It starts with a chocolate crumb crust, is filled with a rich chocolate filling, and has the option of being topped with chocolate shavings. Who said eating healthy isn't fun?*

1	9-inch Chocolate Cheesecake Crumb Crust, page 101	4	Tbs brown sugar
2	cups low-fat cottage cheese	1/4	cup Dutch-process cocoa powder (like Hershey's European)
8	oz tub-style light cream cheese	2	Tbs all-purpose flour
8	oz non-fat cream cheese, room temperature	1	Tbs cornstarch
1/2	cup semi-sweet chocolate chips, melted and cooled	1	tsp vanilla extract
		1/2	tsp almond extract
1 1/2	cups Splenda Granular	1	large egg
		3	large egg whites
		1/2	cup light sour cream

Preheat oven to 350 degrees. Wrap 9-inch springform pan with crust tightly in heavy-duty foil to waterproof.

Place cottage cheese into a food processor or blender. Purée until completely smooth. Spoon into a large mixing bowl and add nonfat and light cream cheeses. Beat on medium speed with an electric mixer until creamy. Add the cooled, melted chocolate, Splenda, brown sugar, cocoa powder, flour, cornstarch, and extracts. Beat on low speed until smooth. Add whole egg and then egg whites, beating briefly after each addition to incorporate. Stir in the sour cream with a large spoon. Pour into the prepared pan and smooth top. Place the foil-wrapped pan in a large, deep baking pan and pour boiling water into pan until it reaches halfway up the outside of the cheesecake pan. Bake for 55 to 60 minutes or until sides of cake appear firm and center jiggles slightly. Turn off heat, open oven door, and let cheesecake cool in the oven for 30 minutes. Remove from water bath and finish cooling. Refrigerate at least 6 hours before serving. *Twelve servings.*

Option: Take one 1.5-oz chocolate bar, and grate or "peel" off curls with the use of a vegetable peeler onto the top of the cake. This beautiful addition only adds 10 calories, 1.5 grams carbs, and 0.5 grams of fat per piece.

Per serving:

Calories 220
Carbohydrate 24 grams (sugar 13)
Protein 13 grams
Fat 8 grams (saturated 5)
Fiber 1 gram
Sodium 380 grams
Diabetic exchange = 1 1/2 carbohydrate, 2 very lean meat

Mocha Chip Cheesecake

*C*offee and chocolate—another great combination. This smooth cheesecake filling is lightly flavored with coffee and studded with miniature chocolate chips. It would make a great addition to any dinner party.

1	9-inch Chocolate Cheesecake Crumb Crust, page 101	1	Tbs cornstarch
1	cup low-fat cottage cheese	½	tsp vanilla extract
8	oz tub-style light cream cheese	1	Tbs + 1 tsp instant coffee powder
8	oz non-fat cream cheese, room temperature	2	Tbs hot water
1½	cups Splenda Granular	2	large eggs
2	Tbs all-purpose flour	2	large egg whites
		2	tsp all-purpose flour
		⅔	cup mini chocolate chips

Preheat oven to 350 degrees. Wrap 9-inch springform pan with crust tightly in heavy-duty foil to waterproof.

Place cottage cheese into a food processor or blender. Purée until completely smooth. Spoon into a large mixing bowl and add nonfat and light cream cheeses. On medium speed with an electric mixer, beat until creamy. Add the Splenda, flour, cornstarch, and vanilla. Beat on low until smooth. Dissolve the coffee in the hot water and add to batter. Add whole eggs and then egg whites, beating briefly after each addition to incorporate. Coat the chocolate chips with the 2 teaspoons of flour and fold in. Pour into the prepared pan and smooth top. Place the foil-wrapped pan in a large, deep baking dish and pour boiling water into pan until it reaches halfway up the outside of the cheesecake pan. Bake for 60 minutes or until sides of cake appear firm and center jiggles slightly. Turn off heat, open oven door, and let cheesecake cool in oven for 30 minutes. Remove from water bath and finish cooling. Refrigerate at least 6 hours before serving. *Twelve servings.*

Per serving:

Calories 220
Carbohydrate 22 grams (sugar 12)
Protein 11 grams
Diabetic exchange = 1½ carbohydrate, 1½ medium fat meat

Fat 10 grams (saturated 6)
Fiber 1 gram
Sodium 350 milligrams

Pumpkin Streusel Cheesecake

This is one of my favorite desserts for the holidays. It looks festive and tastes fabulous. I have made it many times in the past using sugar. I am happy to say that this sugar-free version is just as good as the original.

CRUST

18 gingersnap cookies, ground into crumbs
    (may substitute graham cracker crumbs)
¼ cup Splenda Granular
1 Tbs light margarine or butter, melted

FILLING

1 cup low-fat cottage cheese	1 tsp cinnamon
8 oz tub-style light cream cheese	½ tsp ground ginger
8 oz non-fat cream cheese, room temperature	½ tsp allspice
1¼ cups Splenda Granular	1 tsp vanilla
1 15-oz can solid pack pumpkin	2 large eggs
2 Tbs cornstarch	4 large egg whites
1 Tbs all-purpose flour	½ cup light sour cream

STREUSEL

¼ cup all-purpose flour
1 Tbs brown sugar
1 Tbs light butter, cold

Preheat oven to 350. Spray a 9-inch springform pan with nonstick cooking spray.

In a small bowl combine the cookie crumbs with the Splenda. Add the butter and stir to mix. Reserve ⅓ cup of the crumbs and press rest of crumbs onto the bottom of prepared pan. Bake for 5 minutes. Set aside.

Place cottage cheese into a food processor or blender. Purée until completely smooth. Spoon into a large mixing bowl and add nonfat and light cream cheeses. On medium speed with an electric mixer, beat until creamy. Add the pumpkin, Splenda, flour, cornstarch, spices, and vanilla. Beat on low speed until smooth. Add whole eggs and then egg whites, beating briefly after each addition to incorporate. Stir in the sour cream with a large spoon. Pour into the prepared crust and smooth top. Bake for 75 minutes or until the sides are firm and the center jiggles slightly.

While baking, prepare streusel: Add flour and brown sugar to the reserved cookie crumbs. Cut in butter until a loose crumb forms. After baking cheesecake, open oven and sprinkle crumbs over entire cake (covering any cracks). Place back in oven for an additional 15 minutes. Turn off heat, open door, and let cheesecake cool in oven for 30 minutes. Remove from oven and place on rack to cool. Refrigerate at least 6 hours before serving. Best if made a day or two in advance. *Twelve servings.*

Per serving:

Calories 200

Fat 7 grams (saturated 4)

Carbohydrate 21 grams (sugar 9)

Fiber 2 grams

Protein 11 grams

Sodium 370 milligrams

Diabetic exchange = 1½ carbohydrate, 1½ medium fat meat

Pumpkin Cheesecake is a new Thanksgiving tradition in my home!

Cheesecake Parfait

This is a really fun dessert. The presentation is original, and your family and guests are sure to love it. Besides looking incredible, it's smooth and rich and creamy. You'll love it too, because it's so simple to prepare and yet looks and tastes very impressive. These are also fabulous for entertaining because they are already portioned, and convenient since they can be made ahead of time.

½ cup graham cracker crumbs	½ cup light sour cream
2 Tbs Splenda Granular	¼ cup Splenda Granular
1½ Tbs light butter, melted	1 cup light whipped
4 oz tub-style light cream cheese	topping, thawed
4 ounces non-fat cream cheese, room temperature	1¼ cups fresh blueberries

Select 6 tall-stemmed glasses—an 8-ounce wine glass or champagne glass is ideal. In a small bowl, mix graham cracker crumbs, 2 tablespoons Splenda, and butter. Set aside.

In a medium mixing bowl, beat cream cheeses with an electric mixer until creamy. Add sour cream and ¼ cup Splenda and stir until smooth. Fold in light whipped topping with a spoon or spatula. In the bottom of each glass, place 1 tablespoon graham cracker mix. Press down with spoon. Place about 3 tablespoons of cream cheese mix on top of each. (You will use only half of the cheese mixture for the 6 glasses.) Divide the berries among the glasses, placing them on top of the cream cheese layer. Add one more layer of cream cheese. Finish the parfait by topping each with 1 tablespoon of crumbs.

These can be enjoyed immediately or placed in the refrigerator until ready to be served. *Six servings.*

Per serving:

Calories 185	Fat 8 grams (saturated 6)
Carbohydrate 20 grams (sugar 12)	Fiber 1 gram
Protein 7 grams	Sodium 280 milligrams
Diabetic exchange = 1 carbohydrate, 1 low-fat meat, 1 fat	

The original recipe for these parfaits clocks in at a whopping 490 calories each!

Key Lime Cheesecake

If you like key lime pie, this is the cheesecake for you. It has a lighter texture than most cheesecakes, and of course has the wonderful tartness of key limes. Key lime juice can be found next to the bottled lemon juice in most markets.

1	9-inch Cheesecake Crumb Crust
1	envelope of unflavored gelatin (2½ tsp)
¾	cup key lime juice
2	large eggs, lightly beaten
1	cup Splenda Granular
8	oz tub-style light cream cheese
8	oz non-fat cream cheese, room temperature
4	large pasteurized egg whites (or 2 regular egg whites*)
¾	cup Splenda Granular
1½	cups light whipped topping

*Note: See Eggs on page 27 regarding the safety of raw eggs.

In a medium saucepan, dissolve the gelatin in the key lime juice for three minutes. Add 1 cup of Splenda, and the 2 beaten eggs. Place on stove, turn heat to medium while stirring, and cook for 10 minutes or until mixture thickens. Remove from heat. Cool slightly. Place the cream cheese in a large bowl and beat on medium speed with an electric mixer until creamy. Slowly add the lime mixture and beat on low until smooth. Refrigerate mixture until thoroughly cooled, stirring every 10 minutes. In a separate bowl, beat the egg whites until foamy or until soft peaks begin form; this can take 5 minutes or more with pasteurized egg whites. Slowly add the ¾ cup Splenda until incorporated. Fold egg-white mixture into the chilled lime-cheese mix. Pour onto prepared crust. Refrigerate until set, about 2 hours. Spread whipped topping over cake. *Twelve servings.*

Per serving:

Calories 160
Carbohydrate 16 grams (sugar 6)
Protein 7 grams
Diabetic exchange = 1 carbohydrate, 1 lean meat, 1 fat

Fat 7.5 grams (saturated 4)
Fiber 0 grams
Sodium 270 milligrams

The original recipe of this yummy, sweet, yet tart cheesecake had 40 grams of sugar per piece!

Chocolate Peppermint Cheesecake

*H*ere it is—*your Christmas cheesecake. It's wonderful. It starts with a chocolate crumb crust that is filled with a peppermint-flecked cream cheese mixture. It finishes with crushed peppermint candies and chocolate on the top. No, you are not dreaming, this cheesecake is still low in sugar, fat, and calories. And the best part of all—it's a cinch to make, leaving you free for all your other holiday chores.*

I	Chocolate Cheesecake Crumb Crust, page 101	12	sugar-free peppermint hard candies, finely crushed
I	envelope unflavored gelatin (2½ tsp)	½	tsp peppermint extract
¼	cup cold water	1½	cups light whipped topping, thawed
8	oz tub-style light cream cheese	6	sugar free, peppermint hard candies, crushed
8	ounces non-fat cream cheese, room temperature	I	1.5 ounce milk or semisweet chocolate bar
½	cup Splenda Granular		
½	cup 1% milk		

In a small saucepan, sprinkle the gelatin over water; let stand for 3 minutes. Place over low heat, stirring, until gelatin dissolves. Remove from heat. In a large mixing bowl, with an electric mixer, beat the cream cheeses and Splenda until creamy. Add the gelatin mixture and the milk. Beat on low speed until smooth. Stir in the 12 crushed peppermints and extract. Chill until the mixture mounds slightly when dropped from a spoon. Fold in the whipped topping. Pour into the prepared crust and smooth top.

Refrigerate at least 3 hours. Before serving, sprinkle top of the cake with remaining crushed peppermint candies. As a final decorative touch, use a vegetable peeler to shave chocolate curls directly onto the top of the cake—and wait for the oohs and aahs. ***Ten servings. (I usually cut 12 pieces, but splurge—it's Christmas!)***

Per serving:

Calories 190

Carbohydrate 22 grams (sugar 14)

Protein 8 grams

Fat 8 grams (saturated 5)

Fiber 0 grams

Sodium 320 milligrams

Diabetic exchange = 1½ carbohydrate, 1 lean meat, 1 fat

While the added sugar is slightly higher in this recipe than in others in the book, the total carb count is still incredibly low (less than half of the original version). Add to that the elimination of 30 grams of fat and 340 calories and you've got yourself the type of treat you can easily make room for. I found my sugar-free hard peppermints on the candy aisle of my local grocery store—during the holidays you could also use crushed sugar-free candy canes.

Puddings and Specialty Desserts

*S*ome *desserts seem to be extra-special. They are the ones you rarely, if ever, make, and yet relish every time you eat them. They are often the types of desserts that don't fit into the more common categories of cakes, pies, and cookies. I've included those special recipes in this chapter. Decadent items like cream puffs, mousses, and soufflés. Traditional treats like shortcakes and strudels, and comforting favorites like a bowl of warm pudding. Many of them hold great memories for me—and perhaps for you, too. If you have eliminated these incredible sweets from your diet because of health concerns, you're in luck, because you can truly enjoy these favorites all the time. Every dessert in this chapter has less than 200 calories per serving (The "Marvel-ous" Lemon Mousse has only 100!) and is low in fat and sugar. But what is really incredible is that they look and taste tremendous. Now that is special!*

Vanilla Pudding
Double Chocolate Pudding
Pumpkin Custard Cups
Strawberry "Short" Cake
Amazing Cream Puffs
Apple Strudel
"Marvel-ous" Lemon Mousse
Tiramisu in a Glass
Strawberry Soufflé
Chocolate Mousse "Cake"

Vanilla Pudding

*W*hen it comes to pudding at my house, we have the vanilla camp versus the chocolate camp. I definitely belong to the first camp, especially when it comes to smooth, sweet, creamy puddings like this one. This rich vanilla pudding stands on its own as a prized homestyle dessert, but it can also be used in your favorite parfait recipes, or as filling for a vanilla cream pie.

- **3   Tbs cornstarch**
- **⅔   cup Splenda Granular**
- **½   cup non-fat half-and-half**
- **I   large egg + I egg yolk, slightly beaten**
- **1¾ cups 1% milk**
- **1½ tsp vanilla**

In a medium saucepan, combine the cornstarch, Splenda, non-fat half-and-half and beaten egg. Whisk until smooth. Whisk in 1% milk. Cook and stir over medium heat until the pudding is thick and bubbly. Cook for 1 minute more. Remove from heat. Stir in the vanilla. Pour into medium bowl or divide among 5 dessert dishes. Cover with plastic wrap. Chill. Refrigerate until served. *Five servings.*

Variation: To use as a filling for vanilla cream pie, add 1 additional tablespoon of cornstarch.

Per serving:

Calories 110
Carbohydrate 15 grams (sugar 4)
Protein 4 grams
Diabetic exchange = ½ low-fat milk, ½ carbohydrate

Fat 3 grams (saturated 1)
Fiber 0 grams
Sodium 60 milligrams

Non-fat half-and-half adds richness without fat to this pudding; you may substitute evaporated skim milk or additional 1% milk for non-fat half-and-half.

Double Chocolate Pudding

This pudding is for the chocolate lovers in your household. This rich and creamy chocolate version puts its packaged sugar-free counterparts to shame. A special occasion is not a requirement, but this pudding will make any day seem out of the ordinary.

3   Tbs cornstarch
¾   cup Splenda Granular
2   Tbs Dutch-process cocoa powder (like Hershey's European)
½   cup non-fat half-and-half
I   large egg, slightly beaten
1¾ cups 1% milk
⅓   cup chocolate chips
1½ tsp vanilla

In a medium saucepan, combine the cornstarch, Splenda, cocoa powder, non-fat half-and-half, and large beaten egg. Whisk until smooth. Whisk in 1% milk. Cook and stir over medium heat until the pudding is thick and bubbly. Cook for 1 minute more. Remove from heat. Stir in the chocolate chips, whisking until melted. Stir in vanilla. Pour into medium bowl or divide among 6 dessert dishes. Cover with plastic wrap. Chill. Refrigerate until served. *Six servings.*

Per serving:

Calories 130
Carbohydrate 18 grams (sugar 8)
Protein 4 grams
Diabetic exchange = ½ low-fat milk, ½ carbohydrate, ½ fat

Fat 4.5 grams (saturated 2.5)
Fiber 0 grams
Sodium 65 milligrams

In a tall glass, alternate layers of chocolate and vanilla pudding for a "zebra" parfait.

Pumpkin Custard Cups

The best part of pumpkin pie is the rich pumpkin filling, of course. Here is a recipe that gives you that delicious filling without the added calories and work of a crust. Another bonus—adding an extra egg yolk and baking the filled cups in a water bath produces an even creamier custard texture than you achieve with a pie.

I   recipe pumpkin pie filling, page 72
I   egg yolk

Preheat oven to 350 degrees. Spray seven 6-ounce custard or soufflé cups with nonstick cooking spray.

Prepare the pie filling according to the directions (eliminating the crust and the beaten egg white wash) using 1 additional egg yolk (you can simply substitute 1 additional large whole egg for 1 of the egg whites). Pour the filling into the cups, and place cups in a large, deep baking pan. Pour boiling water into the baking pan until it reaches halfway up the sides of the cups. Bake for 40 minutes or until a knife inserted near the center of the custard comes out clean. *Seven servings.*

Per Serving:

Calories 120
Carbohydrate 17 grams (sugar 10)
Protein 8 grams
Diabetic exchange = 1/2 carbohydrate, 1/2 low-fat milk, 1/2 vegetable

Fat 1.5 grams (saturated 0.5)
Fiber 2 grams
Sodium 100 milligrams

Individual servings are great for portion control.

Strawberry "Short" Cake

*S*trawberry shortcake is always a special treat. What makes this particular cake even better, is that it only takes a "short" time to prepare. Using with a reduced-fat baking mix makes it quick and easy to produce tender, sweet biscuits to hold all those luscious, fresh berries.

4	cups sliced strawberries	½	tsp baking soda
¼	cup Splenda Granular	⅔	cup low-fat buttermilk
2	cups reduced-fat baking mix (like Bisquick Reduced Fat)	1½	Tbs margarine or butter, melted
⅓	cup Splenda Granular	1	egg, beaten
1	tsp baking powder	1	tsp sugar (optional)
		1½	cups light whipped topping, thawed

Preheat oven to 425 degrees. Spray a baking sheet with nonstick cooking spray.

In a medium bowl, toss strawberries and ¼ cup Splenda. Set aside.

In a large bowl combine baking mix, ⅓ cup Splenda, baking powder, and baking soda. Mix buttermilk and melted butter together and pour over dry ingredients. Stir with a spoon until dough comes together. Remove dough from bowl and place on lightly floured surface. Knead dough 10 times, then pat or roll into even half-inch thickness. Using a 2½ inch round cutter or glass, cut out shortcakes and transfer them to the prepared baking sheet. Gather scraps of dough together and cut out more cakes for a total of eight. Brush with beaten egg and sprinkle a little sugar on each cake. Bake for 12 to 15 minutes. Transfer to rack and let cool slightly.

To assemble shortcakes: Split each shortcake in half. Place the bottoms on dessert plates. Cover with ½ cup berries on each cake. Cover with top half of each cake. Spoon 3 tablespoons light whipped topping on top of biscuits and serve immediately. *Eight servings.*

Per serving:

Calories 195
Carbohydrate 31 grams (sugar 8)
Protein 3.5 grams
Diabetic exchange = 1½ carbohydrate, ½ fruit

Fat 6 grams (saturated 3)
Fiber 2 grams
Sodium 420 milligrams

Try substituting fresh peaches or other berries to give an old favorite a new twist.

Amazing Cream Puffs

I'll never forget the first time I made cream puffs. I was nine years old, and my Girl Scout troop made them for a Mother's Day luncheon. I was amazed by the way the small balls of dough puffed up into these gorgeous, brown, airy, shells ready to be filled. These are an extraordinary treat, and although not difficult to make, they require three steps: the puff, the cream filling, and the chocolate fudge topping. You can make the puffs a day ahead, or longer, and freeze them. The filling keeps for one day and the Chocolate Fudge Sauce keeps for a week (unless you eat it sooner). You may prepare the puffs in separate steps if you prefer. However, they are best eaten within a day (this is rarely a problem!).

PUFFS

⅔   cup water
3   Tbs butter
¼   tsp salt
¼   cup all-purpose flour
1   large egg
3   large egg whites

FILLING

1   recipe Vanilla Pudding, page 114
    (eliminate ½ cup non-fat half-and-half from recipe)
½   cup light whipped topping

TOPPING
⅓   cup Chocolate Fudge Sauce, page 132

Preheat oven to 300 degrees. Spray a baking sheet with nonstick cooking spray.

To prepare puffs: In a medium saucepan, bring the water, butter, and salt to a boil. Add flour, all at once, and stir until the mixture is smooth and pulls away from the sides to form a ball. Remove from heat. Let cool 3 minutes. Add egg and then egg whites, beating vigorously after each addition until mixture is smooth and shiny again. Using a tablespoon, spoon dough onto prepared baking pan, making 8 mounds. Place pan in lower third of oven and turn heat up to 450 degrees. Bake 15 minutes, until dough is well puffed and brown. Turn oven back to 300 degrees and bake 15 more minutes. Cut a small slit on the side of each puff to allow steam to escape, turn off heat and allow puffs to dry for 5 minutes in the oven. Remove and place on rack to cool. Once cool, puffs can be kept one day in an airtight container or wrapped well and frozen.

To prepare filling: Allow vanilla pudding to cool according to directions. When cool, add ¼ cup of whipped topping and stir until smooth. Fold in rest of topping. The filling can be kept covered and refrigerated for one day.

Topping: Prepare chocolate fudge sauce according to directions. If prepared in advance, heat lightly to a pourable consistency before using.

To assemble cream puffs: Cut top off each puff. Fill with ¼ cup cream filling and replace top. Drizzle 2 teaspoons of Chocolate Fudge Sauce over the top of each cream puff. *Eight servings.*

Per serving:

Calories 170

Carbohydrate 18 grams (sugar 3)

Protein 6 grams

Fat 8 grams (saturated 4)

Fiber 0 grams

Sodium 70 milligrams

Diabetic exchange = 1 carbohydrate, 1 lean meat, 1 fat

Starting the puffs in a moderate temperature oven and increasing the heat allows the puffs to reach their maximum height. They rise along with the temperature in the oven.

Apple Strudel

Replacing the classic strudel pastry with phyllo dough makes this traditional holiday favorite a snap to put together, and a whole lot healthier to eat. Phyllo (or filo) dough can be found frozen near the pastries in most grocery stores. Be sure to thaw the dough thoroughly before using and to keep the sheets you are not working with covered with a damp cloth or plastic wrap so they will not dry out.

4	cups finely sliced, peeled apples (about 1½–1¾ pounds fresh)
⅓	cup Splenda Granular
¼	cup raisins, finely chopped
¼	cup pecans, finely chopped
1½	tsp cinnamon
1	Tbs plain bread crumbs
6	sheets phyllo dough (16½ × 12 inches)
½	Tbs butter, melted
1	Tbs powdered sugar

Preheat oven to 350 degrees. Spray a baking sheet with nonstick cooking spray.

In a large bowl, combine apples and next 5 ingredients. Set aside.

Spread a large piece of plastic wrap or wax paper onto a large surface. Carefully lay 1 piece of the phyllo dough onto the work surface, with the long side closest to you. Spray the entire sheet with cooking spray. Lay another sheet of dough on top of the first. Spray again. Repeat until all 6 sheets are stacked. Spoon the apple mixture in a long strip across the center of the dough, leaving 3 inches on all sides. Starting with the long side of the dough that is closest to you lift the empty dough up over the apples. Fold side ends and far side of dough up and over the apples to enclose. Carefully, use the paper to help you turn the strudel seam side down onto the prepared baking sheet. Brush with melted butter. Bake 40 to 45 minutes, or until the pastry is golden brown. Cool slightly and sift powdered sugar over entire strudel. Best when served warm. *Eight servings.*

Per serving:

Calories 160	Fat 6 grams (saturated 1)
Carbohydrate 26 grams (sugar 14)	Fiber 3 grams
Protein 2 grams	Sodium 75 milligrams
Diabetic exchange = 1 fruit, ½ carbohydrate, 1 fat	

> Phyllo dough is lower in fat and carbohydrate than other pastry doughs.

"Marvel-ous" Lemon Mousse

I call this "marvel-ous" because this recipe is a marvel of good nutrition. It is filled with things that are good for you, like protein, vitamin C, and calcium. And it's all packed into 100 slim calories. Cool, creamy, and sweet with a nice tart touch of lemon, you'd never guess it's so good for you!

1	envelope unflavored gelatin
⅔	cup lemon juice
¾	cup Splenda Granular
	finely grated zest of 1 lemon
2	drops yellow food coloring (optional)
½	cup cottage cheese
8	ounces non-fat plain yogurt
1	egg white, pasteurized
1	Tbs sugar
¾	cup light whipped topping

Place the gelatin in a small saucepan. Add ⅓ cup of the lemon juice and let stand for 3 minutes. Place on low heat and add remaining ⅓ cup of lemon juice, Splenda, zest and food coloring if desired. Heat for 3 to 4 minutes until gelatin is completely dissolved. Transfer mixture to a bowl. Set aside and allow to cool slightly. Stir occasionally so mixture does not gel. Purée cottage cheese and yogurt until completely smooth. Whisk purée into the lemon-gelatin mixture. Place mixture in the refrigerator to cool, whisking occasionally to prevent lumps. Beat the egg white to soft peaks. Add a tablespoon of sugar and beat until stiff, but not dry. Fold into the cooled lemon mixture. Fold in light whipped topping. *Six servings.*

Per serving:

Calories 100
Carbohydrate 13 grams (sugar 8)
Protein 9 grams
Diabetic exchange = 1 very low-fat milk

Fat 1.5 grams (saturated 1)
Fiber 0 grams
Sodium 55 milligrams

Top with Strawberry or Blueberry Coulis (pages 129 and 130) for an elegant dessert.

Tiramisu in a Glass

*T*iramisu *is a beloved Italian dessert. The best versions contain a rich, smooth, Italian cream cheese, called mascarpone. Unfortunately, this specialty cheese is loaded with fat. Combine this with the usual cream, egg yolks, and sugar traditionally used to make tiramisu, and you have one heavy dessert. In this recipe I have kept in some of the mascarpone for its unique flavor, but have lightened the additional ingredients to create an incredible rich-tasting dessert. I also have chosen a unique and contemporary way to serve the dessert by assembling individual portions in martini glasses. However, you may assemble it by layering the ingredients in a large serving dish as described below.*

4	oz mascarpone cheese*
4	oz non-fat cream cheese
1/4	cup low-fat ricotta cheese
2	Tbs light sour cream
1/2	cup Splenda Granular
3/4	cup light whipped topping
3/4	cup water
1	Tbs instant coffee
3	Tbs Splenda Granular
1	Tbs brandy (optional)
1	3-oz package ladyfingers (need 12 split fingers)
1	tsp Dutch-process cocoa powder (like Hershey's European)
1/2	oz semisweet chocolate, shaved (optional)

*You can substitute 4 ounces light tub-style cream cheese and 2 tablespoons light sour cream.

Gather 6 standard martini glasses (about 6 ounces each) or a 1-quart serving dish. In a medium mixing bowl, beat the mascarpone and the next 4 ingredients with an electric mixer until creamy and smooth. Fold in the light whipped topping. Set aside.

Place the water in a small microwaveable bowl or saucepan. Add the instant coffee and Splenda—and brandy, if desired—and heat for 2 minutes.

To assemble individual tiramisus: For each tiramisu, lightly dip the outside of 4 ladyfinger pieces (2 whole ladyfingers, each split in half), in coffee mixture and place standing up against the sides of the martini glass. Brush the inside of the ladyfingers with more coffee. Place 1/2 cup of cheese mixture in the center of the ladyfingers. Sift small amount (1/8 teaspoon) of the cocoa powder over the cheese mixture, Top with a touch of shaved chocolate, if desired. Wrap glass with plastic wrap and refrigerate for 6 hours before serving.

To assemble in a single dish: Place half of the ladyfingers on the bottom of the dish. Brush ladyfingers with half of the coffee mixture. Top with half of the cheese mixture and smooth.

Repeat. Sift the cocoa powder over the top of the tiramisu. Top with the shaved chocolate, if desired. Refrigerate for 6 hours before serving. *Six servings.*

Per serving:

Calories 160
Carbohydrate 9 grams (sugar 3)
Protein 5 grams
Diabetic exchange = ½ carbohydrate, 1 very lean meat, 2 fat

Fat 11 grams (saturated 4.5)
Fiber 0 grams
Sodium 135 milligrams

The percentage of calories from fat is slightly higher in this rich-tasting treat, but the total is still quite low. On the other hand, my traditional tiramisu recipe has 460 calories, 34 grams of sugar, and 43 grams of fat per serving. Mama Mia!

Strawberry Soufflé

*T*his is one of the first recipes I developed for the book. I made it and took it to a dinner party. Everyone loved it. My friends commented on how light and creamy it was. They also noted the fresh strawberry flavor. What they did not comment on was the fact that the sugar was replaced with Splenda. This told me what I really wanted to know—that Splenda could sweeten my favorite desserts with the wonderful taste of sugar.

2	pints of fresh strawberries (approximately 2 pounds)	6	large egg whites or 10 pasteurized egg whites
2	envelopes unflavored gelatin (2½ tsp each)	¼	cup Splenda Granular
¼	cup Splenda Granular	1	8-oz container light whipped topping, thawed
1	Tbs lemon juice		

Set aside a 2-quart soufflé dish or bowl.

Clean, stem, and halve berries. You should have about 5 cups. Reserve four berries for garnish.

Purée the remaining berries in a food processor or blender. Place 1 cup of purée in a medium saucepan. Add gelatin and ¼ cup Splenda. Heat until gelatin dissolves. Add the rest of the purée and the lemon juice. Remove from heat and chill for 20 minutes. While purée is chilling, beat egg whites until foamy. Add Splenda and continue to beat until stiff but not dry. Fold ¼ of the egg whites into the cooled purée. Gently fold in the remaining egg whites. Fold in the light whipped topping. Spoon into the soufflé dish and chill in the refrigerator for at least 4 hours before serving.

Just before serving, garnish the top of the soufflé with the reserved berries. *Eight servings.*

Per serving:

Calories 120
Carbohydrate 16 grams (sugar 10)
Protein 5 grams
Diabetic exchange = 1 medium fat meat, ½ fruit

Fat 4 grams (saturated 3.5)
Fiber 1 gram
Sodium 45 milligrams

The beaten egg whites are crucial to the lightness and volume of the soufflé. In order to achieve the greatest egg white volume with the fewest eggs, I use regular egg whites. If you do the same, be sure to use fresh eggs that are clean and have been inspected for cracks. When preparing this dessert for children, the elderly, or those with compromised immune systems, be sure to use the pasteurized egg whites.

Chocolate Mousse "Cake"

*M*y *parents happened to be in town the day I made this cake. After dinner, I served it to my father, a lover of all things rich, sweet, and fattening. When I asked him what he thought, he answered with one word, "decadent." Unlike most cakes, this incredible dessert has the light and creamy, yet rich, texture of mousse. It sits on a chocolate crumb crust, and unlike mousse, it can be sliced like a cake. Thus, I call it a mousse "cake." My dad prefers to call it "perfect."*

CRUST

3/4	cup chocolate graham cracker crumbs
1	Tbs Splenda Granular
1	tsp unsweetened Dutch-process cocoa powder (like Hershey's European)
1 1/2	Tbs margarine

FILLING

1	envelope unsweetened gelatin (2 1/2 tsp)
1/4	cup water
1	cup 1% milk
1	large egg, lightly beaten
1/3	cup unsweetened Dutch-process cocoa powder
2/3	cup Splenda Granular
1/3	cup semi-sweet chocolate chips
1	tsp vanilla
1/4	tsp orange extract or 1 Tbs orange liqueur
3	large pasteurized egg whites (2 if using regular eggs*)
1	Tbs sugar
1	cup light whipped topping, thawed
1/2	oz chocolate shavings (optional)

*See Eggs, on page 27, regarding the safety of raw eggs.

Preheat oven to 350 degrees. Spray a 9-inch springform pan with non-stick cooking spray.

In a small bowl, combine the graham cracker crumbs, Splenda, and cocoa powder. Add the margarine and stir to mix. Press crumbs onto bottom and 1 1/2 inches up the sides of the prepared pan (pressing with plastic wrap will help with the sides). Bake for 8 minutes. Cool.

In a medium saucepan, sprinkle gelatin over 1/4 cup of water. Let stand 3 minutes. Whisk in milk, beaten egg, cocoa powder, and Splenda. Place on stove and turn heat to medium. Cook, stirring until thickened and smooth. Add chocolate chips and stir until melted. Stir in vanilla and orange extract. Remove from heat. Pour into a large bowl and let cool. Refrigerate for 30 minutes, stirring occasionally until mixture is cold and begins to mound when dropped from a spoon.

Beat egg whites until frothy. Add sugar and continue to beat until stiff, but not dry. Fold egg whites into chocolate mixture. Fold in light whipped topping. Pour mousse into crust and smooth. Refrigerate for at least 2 hours. Garnish with a touch of chocolate shavings, if desired. *Eight servings.*

Per serving:

Calories 175
Carbohydrate 24 grams (sugar 14)
Protein 5 grams
Fat 7.5 grams (saturated 3.5)
Fiber 1.5 grams
Sodium 130 milligrams
Diabetic exchange = 1 carbohydrate, 1 lean meat, 1 fat

Simple Sauces and Toppings

*H*ow do you make an ordinary dessert extraordinary? Just add a sauce or a topping. Sauces and toppings are a great way to create, dress up, or embellish your favorite treats. What I love about them, besides how professional they make everything look, is how easy they are to make and keep, and how little it takes to really jazz up any dessert. Unfortunately, with most sauces or toppers, that "little" embellishment really adds to the sugar, fat, and caloric content of the dessert. Not here, of course. These scrumptious sauces and toppings add a whole lot more pleasure to the dessert than to the numbers in the nutritional analysis. The Berry Sauces are fresh tasting and versatile, and can be used on everything from plain cakes to ice cream and cheesecakes. The Rich Custard Sauce takes fruit to a whole new level. Lemon Curd is a basic for fillings and frostings. Chocolate Fudge Sauce is terrific on just about everything (even on a spoon!). Last, but not least, the Orange Cream Cheese is the perfect complement to breads or muffins and the Easy Chocolate Cream Frosting can dress up a chocolate cake or turn Chocolate Chocolate Chip Muffins into truly dangerous treats!

Rich Custard Sauce
Blueberry Sauce and Coulis
Strawberry Sauce and Coulis
Quick Raspberry Sauce
Chocolate Fudge Sauce
Lemon Curd
Orange Cream Cheese
Easy Chocolate Cream Frosting

Rich Custard Sauce

I love fresh fruit, especially berries. But fresh fruit for dessert, well—it's still just fresh fruit. Now, place some berries in a nice glass, pour on a little Rich Custard sauce and voilà—real dessert. So simple, so good! You can also add a little orange zest and use this sauce on simple cakes like the Citrus Chiffon Cake or your favorite angel food cake.

2   **Tbs Splenda Granular**
I   **Tbs cornstarch**
2   **egg yolks**
I   **cup 1% milk**
¼   **cup non-fat half-and-half**
I ½ **tsp vanilla**

Place Splenda, cornstarch, and egg yolks in a small saucepan. Whisk together until eggs have lightened in color and Splenda and cornstarch are dissolved. Whisk in milk and half-and-half.

Place pan on stove and turn heat to medium. Heat, stirring constantly, until mixture comes to a low boil. Turn heat down and let simmer 1 minute. Custard should be thick enough to coat a spoon but not as thick as pudding. Whisk in vanilla. Pour into a bowl and cover with plastic wrap. Cool and refrigerate until ready to serve. *Nine servings (2 tablespoons each).*

Per serving:

Calories 35
Carbohydrate 3 grams (sugar 1)
Protein 2 grams
Diabetic exchange = ¼ low-fat milk

Fat 1.5 grams (saturated 0.5)
Fiber 0 grams
Sodium 15 milligrams

Add a touch of orange zest or a tablespoon of orange liqueur when serving over fresh strawberries for a delicious treat.

Blueberry Sauce and Coulis

This would make a lovely gift. Once made and bottled, it will hold for up to two weeks in the refrigerator. It's a wonderful complement to lemon desserts as well as good old vanilla ice cream.

2	cups fresh or frozen blueberries (I pint)
1/4	cup Splenda Granular
1/3	cup cold water
2	tsp cornstarch
I	tsp lemon juice
I	Tbs crème de cassis liqueur (optional)

Place the berries in a heavy, non-aluminum saucepan. Add remaining ingredients (except liqueur) and stir until cornstarch dissolves. Place over medium heat and bring to a boil. Turn down and simmer for 1 minute, stirring constantly. Remove from heat and stir in liqueur if desired. *Eight servings (3 tablespoons each).*

Variation: For Blueberry Coulis, strain the blueberry sauce through a fine strainer or sieve, pressing on the fruit to drain all the liquid. Throw away pulp. This reduces serving size to 2 tablespoons.

Per serving:

Calories 20
Carbohydrate 5 grams (sugar 3)
Protein 0 grams
Diabetic exchange = I free food

Fat 0 grams (saturated 0)
Fiber I gram
Sodium 0 milligrams

A Coulis is a smooth or puréed sauce of fruit or vegetables.

Strawberry Sauce and Coulis

This is one of the most versatile sauces I know of. Unstrained, it makes a nice chunky sauce for ice cream or plain cakes. Strained, it makes a smooth fruit sauce, or coulis, that is an elegant accompaniment to desserts such as the Heavenly Cheesecake or Strawberry Souffle.

2	cups strawberries, fresh or frozen
1/3	cup Splenda Granular
1	Tbs lemon juice
1/2	cup water
2	tsp cornstarch
1	Tbs orange liqueur (optional)

Place the berries in a heavy, non-aluminum saucepan. Add remaining ingredients (except liqueur) and stir until cornstarch dissolves. Place over medium heat and bring to a boil. Turn down and simmer for 1 minute, stirring constantly. Remove from heat and stir in liqueur if desired.

Variation: For smooth Strawberry Coulis, strain the strawberry sauce through a fine strainer or sieve, pressing on the fruit to drain all the liquid. Throw away pulp. *Eight servings (2 tablespoons each).*

Per serving:

Calories 15
Carbohydrate 3 grams (sugar 1)
Protein 0 grams
Diabetic exchange = 1 free food

Fat 0 grams (saturated 0)
Fiber 0 grams
Sodium 0 grams

> For a dramatic and elegant dessert presentation, Strawberry Coulis can be drizzled, pooled, or painted onto plates before adding dessert.

Quick Raspberry Sauce

It doesn't get any quicker than this. No fancy ingredients are required for this easy sauce, whipped up in the microwave with raspberry jam in just seconds. Drizzle it over cakes or on cake plates for dramatic presentations, or simply use it on your favorite ice cream.

- **6   Tbs low-sugar raspberry jam**
- **6   Tbs water**
- **¼   cup Splenda Granular**

Place all the in ingredients in a small microwaveable bowl. Heat for 30 to 45 seconds on high.

Stir until smooth. Use warm or cold. *Eight servings (1 1/2 tablespoons each).*

Per serving:

Calories 16
Carbohydrate 4 (sugar 3)
Protein 0 grams
Diabetic exchange = 1 free food

Fat 0 grams (saturated 0)
Fiber 0 grams
Sodium 0 milligrams

Chocolate Fudge Sauce

This recipe made my day. I had tried other low-sugar fudge sauce recipes and was never quite satisfied because they were all missing the characteristic texture that sugar imparts. Then I saw a recipe that used maple syrup in place of sugar that piqued my interest. After trying the recipe (using Low-Calorie Log Cabin Syrup made with Splenda) and making a few modifications, success was finally at hand! Just like the best fudge sauces, this tightens up in the refrigerator. Heat gently, in the microwave or on the stove, before using.

2	ounces semi-sweet chocolate
2	Tbs Dutch-process cocoa powder (like Hershey's European)
2	Tbs sugar-free syrup (Log Cabin brand)
1/4	cup Splenda Granular
1/4	cup water
1/2	tsp vanilla

Chop semi-sweet chocolate into small pieces. Place in a medium size microwaveable bowl. (You may also make this in a saucepan on the stove.) Add remaining ingredients. Place in the microwave on high and heat for 45 seconds; chocolate will not be completely melted. Remove and stir thoroughly until smooth. Add vanilla. Makes 3/4 cup. *Twelve servings (1 tablespoon each).*

Per serving:

Calories 30
Carbohydrate 4 grams (sugar 0)
Protein 0 grams
Diabetic exchange = 1/2 fat

Fat 2 grams (saturated 1)
Fiber 0 grams
Sodium 0 milligrams

Compare to Hershey's Chocolate Fudge Topping: It has 70 calories per tablespoon and 10 grams of sugar.

Lemon Curd

*T*his is a filling or topping that can easily be converted to a sauce. It is often used in place of jam on biscuits and as a filling cakes or tarts. I use it to make a luscious lemon cream frosting for the Lemon Coconut Layer Cake on page 95. If you would like to make a thick lemon sauce, simply thin the curd with some hot water and stir until smooth.

- ⅔ cup lemon juice
- 2   Tbs water
- I   large egg, beaten
- I   large egg yolk
- 2   Tbs cornstarch
- ⅔ cup Splenda Granular
- 2   Tbs light butter

In a medium non-aluminum saucepan thoroughly whisk together the first 6 ingredients. Place pan on stove and turn heat to medium. Cook, whisking constantly, until mixture comes to a boil. Boil, whisking, for 1 minute. Mixture should be thick and clear. Remove from the heat and stir in the butter. Cool. *Fourteen servings (1 tablespoon each).*

Per serving:

Calories 25
Carbohydrate 4 grams (sugar 0)
Protein 0 grams
Diabetic exchange = ¼ carbohydrate

Fat 1.5 grams (saturated 0.5)
Fiber 0 grams
Sodium 0 grams

> Mix a couple of tablespoons of lemon curd into softened light cream cheese for a delicious spread that can be used on muffins and biscuits.

Orange Cream Cheese

I served this with the Pumpkin Pecan Bread, page 52, to all my tasters—and it was a huge hit. It would compliment most fruit and bran muffins as well as biscuits or mini-bagels.

4   oz light tub-style cream cheese
1   Tbs orange juice
2   tsp Splenda Granular
1   tsp grated orange zest

Place all the ingredients in a small bowl and beat until creamy. Keeps well in the refrigerator for 1 to 2 weeks. *Eight servings (1 tablespoon each).*

Per serving:

Calories 30
Carbohydrate 1.5 grams (sugar 1)
Protein 1 gram
Diabetic exchange = $\frac{1}{2}$ fat

Fat 2.5 grams (saturated 1)
Fiber 0 grams
Sodium 65 grams

So much tastier than butter with only $\frac{1}{3}$ of the calories and a fraction of the saturated fat.

Easy Chocolate Cream Frosting

This is a quick way to turn light whipped topping into a nice chocolate top-ping or frosting. The recipe makes enough to frost a nine-inch round or square cake or a dozen cupcakes.

1¾ cups light whipped topping, thawed
2   Tbs Dutch-process cocoa powder (like Hershey's European0
¼ cup Splenda Granular

Place whipped topping in a medium bowl. Gently fold in the cocoa powder and Splenda. Overmixing will break down cream topping. Refrigerate until use. May be spread or spooned onto cakes or muffins. *Nine servings (2 tablespoons each).*

Per serving:

Calories 35
Carbohydrate 4 grams (sugar 1)
Protein 0 grams
Diabetic exchange = ½ carbohydrate

Fat 1.5 grams (saturated 1.5)
Fiber 0 grams
Sodium 0 milligrams

Index

Acknowledgements

First and foremost, thanks to my husband, Chuck, and boys, Stephen and James. The messy kitchen, the long hours, and the endless tasting—I couldn't have done it without their constant love and support. Special thanks are in order for my stepdaughter, Colleen, for assisting me and helping me understand how important it is to still fit the foods you love into your meal plan. I am so pleased that I can finally make her great treats! And to the rest of my family: brothers, sisters, and in-laws—thanks for the encouragement.

I am also eternally grateful to my editor, PJ Dempsey, who has been nothing but patient, enthusiastic, supportive, helpful, generous with her time, and always a joy to talk to during this project. It clearly could never have happened without her.

I am also grateful to all the chefs that have helped me understand the importance of great taste, particularly Chef George Hirsch for allowing me to assist on his book, *Living It Up*.

I am also indebted to Carol Kizer, Chairperson of the Hospitality Management Program at Columbus State College for her assistance in my career as a culinary educator.

Professionally, as well as personally, I extend my gratitude to Chef Carolyn Claycomb of the Columbus Culinary Academy for her support and wisdom of all things cooking, and to friend and colleague Krista Kriegel, Director of Nutrition Services for the Central Ohio Diabetes Association, for her professional advice and consultation on all of the information relating to diabetes.

Writing your first book is exciting, but can be very daunting as well. I am very fortunate to have good friends who were willing to step in and help, especially Cheryl Luntz, whose discerning eye for detail proved invaluable in helping proofread the manuscript, and her beautiful daughter Elizabeth who became my number-one kitchen helper. To Cindy Whitley and my super taster Chris Wieland for listening to me endlessly, baking recipes, and giving great feedback. Thanks to John Luntz, Marcie Jundt, Rick and Debra Carey, Pat Bowman, Mary Beth Comfort, and everyone else who was willing taste and critique the recipes with useful and encouraging feedback.

Lastly, some very special people in my life that I can depend on, day in and day out, to be in my corner with unwavering love and support—I thank my Mom and Dad and my closest and dearest friend, Nancie Crosby. Thanks for being there.

About the Author

Marlene Koch, R.D., is a culinary nutritionist who specializes in good health and good food. As a cooking instructor, nutrition educator, and registered dietitian, Marlene combines her love for great-tasting food with her knowledge of nutrition to teach others the art of healthy living. Her clients have included the American Culinary Federation (the national association of Chefs), the Columbus Culinary Academy, the Central Ohio Diabetes Association, and Williams-Sonoma. She also provided her nutritional expertise to public television's Chef George Hirsch in his latest book, *Living It Up*. Marlene can be found in Dublin, Ohio, where she resides with her two energetic sons and her husband, who states that the best place to find delicious, healthy food is "at home." She can also be reached on the internet as a counselor for dietwatch.com.

If you have comments or a healthy Splenda recipe
you would like to share, you may send it to:

Marlene Koch
c/o PJ Dempsey, Senior Editor
M. Evans and Company, Inc.
216 East 49th Street
New York, NY 10017-1502

Original recipes will be considered for future publications
with all rights retained by the author and publisher.